# The Perils of Un-Coordinated Healthcare

T0251987

Despite its frequency and its potential severity, preventable medical harm is still prevalent in American hospitals and continues to put an alarming number of lives at risk, being the third leading cause of death in the United States. Even some of the most commonly performed surgeries, such as knee and hip replacements, are resulting in a rapidly increasing rate of surgical site infections.

Patricia Morrill's book is written specifically for the healthcare industry. It fills the need for exposing how preventable harm is a systemwide problem and provides a step-by-step model to apply for raising process improvement to a strategic level. The approach is ideal for team training purposes. *The Perils of Un-Coordinated Healthcare* gives the reader both a personal and professional view of the impact of preventable medical harm, using case studies and observations on preventable deaths and healthcare practice alongside recommended research topics and resources. By looking at the work of both healthcare workers and their managing executives, this instructional text gives methods to assess workforces and self-assess the performances of managers.

Morrill's ten-step model of *Process Improvement Strategy Deployment* integrates Lean and project management methodologies for developing a problem-solving culture and initiating process improvement at a strategic level. It is essential reading for those in the healthcare industry.

**Patricia W. Morrill** is a project management professional, Lean and Six Sigma certified, and accredited in Evidence-Based Design. She is the president of PM Healthcare Consulting, LLC, where she partners with executives to provide comprehensive coaching and training to lead change and raise process improvement to a strategic level.

# The Perils of Un-Coordinated Healthcare

A Strategic Approach toward
Eliminating Preventable Harm

**Patricia W. Morrill**

Routledge
Taylor & Francis Group

LONDON AND NEW YORK

First published 2017
by Routledge
2 Park Square, Milton Park, Abingdon, Oxon OX14 4RN

and by Routledge
711 Third Avenue, New York, NY 10017

*Routledge is an imprint of the Taylor & Francis Group, an informa business*

© 2017 Patricia W. Morrill

*British Library Cataloguing-in-Publication Data*
A catalogue record for this book is available from the British Library

*Library of Congress Cataloging-in-Publication Data*
Names: Morrill, Patricia, author.
Title: The perils of un-coordinated healthcare : a strategic approach toward
    eliminating preventable harm / Patricia Morrill.
Description: Abingdon, Oxon ; New York, NY : Routledge, [2017] |
    Includes bibliographical references and index.
Identifiers: LCCN 2016052836 | ISBN 9781138228221 (hardback) |
    ISBN 9781138228238 (pbk.) | ISBN 9781315393063 (ebook)
Subjects: | MESH: Process Assessment (Health Care)—methods |
    Patient Harm—prevention & control | Preventive Health Services—
    methods | United States
Classification: LCC RT51 | NLM W 84.4 AA1 | DDC 610.73—dc23
LC record available at https://lccn.loc.gov/2016052836

ISBN: 978-1-138-22822-1 (hbk)
ISBN: 978-1-138-22823-8 (pbk)
ISBN: 978-1-315-39306-3 (ebk)

Typeset in Times New Roman
by Apex CoVantage, LLC

to the memory of my mother
the embodiment of *Live Laugh Love*
who continues to teach so many

&

to my sister
for serving as my editor and cheerleader

# Contents

# Figures

# Tables

# About the author

Patricia W. Morrill, PMP, EDAC, is President of PM Healthcare Consulting, LLC. She specializes in project management and process improvement strategies, coaching and training executives and staff to develop a problem solving culture and lead change. She has over thirty years of healthcare experience and has successfully lead large-scale change initiatives.

Patricia is credentialed in Project Management (PMP), Lean Healthcare, and Six Sigma Green Belt. She is a Senior Member of ASQ serving in leadership positions and a Professional Affiliate with the Center for Health Design, accredited in Evidence-Based Design (EDAC). A Professional Member of the National Speakers Association, Patricia serves as faculty at national conferences and enjoys teaching in the classroom and via webinars. With her vast experience in healthcare and her training in Lean and Project Management, she is passionate about picking up the pace of improvement. She authored the 10-step *Process Improvement Strategy Deployment* model (© 2012), as described in this book, to enhance performance in driving change.

She lives in Wisconsin with her husband and working pet therapy dog.

Contact Patricia at www.pmhcconsulting.com.

# Foreword

I met Patricia Morrill in 2000 when I was the chief quality officer at a health system in Wisconsin and she was the director of project management and the Pebble Project liaison to the Center for Health Design. Our paths crossed as we were both involved in the planning and design phase of two of our hospitals. Early on, I witnessed Patricia's impressive talent for managing complex projects and her intensive work ethic. She not only left no stone unturned as she managed the project but she searched for and found stones that most of us didn't even know existed. We soon became friends and I learned of her passion for ensuring that the healthcare environments that we build have a positive impact on the care that is delivered in them.

Our career paths then diverged, but as it turned out, both of us pursued parallel and complementary interests. I progressed through several physician executive roles, always feeding my obsession with medical error reduction and safe patient care and eventually consulting in the field of healthcare quality, high reliability, and patient safety. Patricia added to an already impressive resume by obtaining high-level credentials in Lean, Six Sigma, project management, and Evidence-Based Design. She moved to an architecture firm where she assisted healthcare clients across the country in the redesign of operational processes and the creation of safe, healing environments. In 2011 she formed her own consulting firm and continues that work as well as writing and speaking extensively on these topics.

Fate then brought these two consultants together in early 2016 and through several delightful meetings we filled each other in on our activities. I was intrigued to learn of her work on the book that you hold in your hands and honored to be allowed to review the manuscript. I was even more thrilled when Patricia asked me to write the foreword and I accepted immediately.

I'd like to give you a sense of the journey that you are about to embark on as Patricia shares her family's personal experience of medical error and integrates that with her own deep understanding of the healthcare system and its shortcomings. The book is divided into two parts, beginning with a deeply emotional and intensely personal story of the events leading up to the death of her mother seven months after an elective knee replacement. The reader will marvel at the way Patricia weaves her private feelings and emotions into the fabric of her process improvement expertise. Writing this book must have reopened many tender emotional wounds. We are the beneficiaries of that labor of love, as her mother's story becomes the foundation for a comprehensive analysis of what went wrong in her case and the impact that the care system has on the patient and her family. Following the case study in Chapter 1, the book is structured as a discussion guide suitable for a group or team environment. She closes out Part One with an exploration of the role of the care providers themselves, the nurses, doctors, and other professionals who operate within a broken system. She explores the impact that the system of care has on them, as well as how these human factors influence a patient's care experience.

After relating the story of "Mother's" death, the book shifts gears and proceeds in Part Two as a detailed syllabus intended to help the reader learn from the errors that occurred. It is designed to serve as a discussion guide and is perfectly suited for a team to work through the various chapters. Extensive references and suggested further reading expands the experience even more.

It challenges us with pointed questions that will stimulate teams to develop their own answers. After sharing insights regarding healthcare management and leadership, Ms. Morrill introduces her own management improvement system, the 10-step model of *Process Improvement Strategy Deployment*, and walks us through its use.

This unique volume successfully combines the personal emotions that are unique to the healthcare industry with a deep knowledge of the science of performance improvement in a format that stimulates discussion and fosters the development of solutions. I am certain that, using this book as a guide, you and your team will derive enhanced sensitivity to the human side of our work along with new ideas to improve your outcomes. Both are worthy goals, and I am grateful to Patricia for sharing her story and her insights on behalf of all of our future patients.

*James Ketterhagen, MD, MMM, CPE,*
*FAAPL, FACS, FACHE*
President & CEO, JK Partners, LLC
jkett@me.com

# Preface

What does coordinated care through the continuum really look like? Until there is an understanding in every healthcare organization about the impact of un-coordinated care, patients – and their families – will suffer.

The intent of this guidebook is twofold: (1) to share case studies to generate discussion and (2) to describe a management improvement system to apply in your organization by raising process improvement to a strategic level.

With over thirty years' experience in the healthcare industry in a career focused on blending operational efficiencies with healing environments, I was stunned and heartbroken by what happened to my own mother, the patient in Chapter 1's story. I have achieved some solace in the knowledge that her case, with its negative outcome, can be used to illustrate methods in problem solving and integrating Lean with project management to bring about greater depths of change.

My sister and I experienced our mother's fully preventable medical conditions: witnessing a serious medication error, a pressure ulcer that wouldn't heal, an infection from knee replacement surgery that couldn't be cured . . . and our mother died.

Our federal government's *Partnership for Patients,* established in 2011, initially revealed nine patient safety areas of focus. Mother suffered from three of those categories: adverse drug event (ADE), pressure ulcer, and surgical site infection (CMS, "Patient Safety Areas of Focus"); plus readmissions, the tenth area of focus added later.

I hope you will learn from Mother's story. It is up to every one of us who use healthcare services to be advocates for ourselves and our loved ones, and it is the responsibility of all healthcare professionals who care for patients to be role models for coordinated care.

## Why does this matter?

As reported by the Institute of Medicine's "To Err is Human: Building a Safer Health System" in November 1999:

> Health care in the United States is not as safe as it should be – and can be. At least 44,000 people, and perhaps as many as 98,000 people, die in hospitals

each year as a result of medical errors that could have been prevented, according to estimates from two major studies.

(National Academy of Sciences 2000)

In a press release, "Medicare Takes New Steps to Help Make Your Hospital Stay Safer," on August 4, 2008:

To encourage hospitals to avoid hospital-acquired conditions, beginning October 1, 2008, Medicare will no longer pay hospitals at a higher rate for the increased costs of care that result when a patient is harmed by one of the listed conditions if it was hospital-acquired.

(CMS 2008)

In "Death by Medical Mistakes Hit Records," published in July 2014:

Preventable medical errors persist as the No. 3 killer in the U.S. – third only to heart disease and cancer – claiming the lives of some 400,000 people each year.

(McCann 2014)

In "Study Suggests Medical Errors Now Third Leading Cause of Death in the U.S.," published in May 2016:

Share Fast Facts:

- 10 percent of all U.S. deaths are now due to medical error.
- Third highest cause of death in the U.S. is medical error.
- Medical errors are an under-recognized cause of death.

(*Johns Hopkins Medicine* 2016)

Clearly it is difficult, if not impossible, to calculate an exact number of preventable medical errors. Whatever the number, we must all agree that it is too high and not tolerable. We must make strategic-level changes to eliminate preventable harm.

*Patricia Morrill*

## Bibliography

Centers for Medicare & Medicaid Services (CMS). "Patient Safety Areas of Focus." Accessed August 7, 2016. https://partnershipforpatients.cms.gov/about-the-partnership/what-is-the-partnership-about/lpwhat-the-partnership-is-about.html

Centers for Medicare & Medicaid Services (CMS). August 4, 2008. "Medicare Takes New Steps to Help Make Your Hospital Stay Safer." Accessed August 9, 2016. https://www.cms.gov/Newsroom/MediaReleaseDatabase/Fact-sheets/2008-Fact-sheets-items/2008–08-045.html?DLPage=1&DLFilter=hospital%20care&DLSort=0&DLSortDir=descending

Johns Hopkins Medicine. 2016. "Study Suggests Medical Errors Now Third Leading Cause of Death in the U.S." http://www.hopkinsmedicine.org/news/media/releases/study_ suggests_medical_e rrors_now_third_leading_cause_of_death_in_the_us

Makary, Martin A. and Michael Daniel. 2016. "Medical Error – The Third Leading Cause of Death in the US." *BMJ*, 353(i2139). doi:10.1136/bmj.i2139

McCann, Erin. July 18, 2014. "Deaths by Medical Mistakes Hit Records." *Healthcare IT News*. Accessed August 7, 2016. http://www.healthcareitnews.com/news/deaths-by-medical-mistakes-hit-records

National Academy of Sciences. 2000. "To Err Is Human Report Brief." Accessed August 9, 2016. http://nationalacademies.org/hmd/~/media/Files/Report%20Files/1999/To-Err-is-Human/To%20Err%20is%20Human%201999%20%20report%20brief.pdf

# Acknowledgements

I could not have completed this book without my cheerleader – my sister. She served as my editor, a much-needed role with this tough subject. She kept encouraging me to get this published.

My husband, daughter, son and close friends have patiently listened to me through the years and through different manuscript versions. They always made me feel that the book was important and urged me to keep at it.

I appreciate my two family members and friend sharing information about their appendectomies, and my husband sharing his open heart surgery experience.

Monroe Clinic was my first client when I started my own consulting firm four months after my mother's death. Without their words of appreciation for sharing real patient scenarios from Mother's story as part of their training, I would not have started to write this book to share with you. I did not realize at the time that my consulting work, making un-coordinated care and preventable harm discussable, would help my own grieving process.

I was honored when a former colleague and friend presented me with the perfect title for this book, demonstrating that she fully understood its purpose. Clinical edits and Foreword by Dr. Jim Ketterhagen, who shares my passion for reducing harm, felt like a stamp of approval for the value this work will have for healthcare teams.

I am so grateful for all the support, encouragement, and assistance I have received from so many. Thank you!

# Part I

# The perils of un-coordinated healthcare

# 1 A case study: the impact of preventable harm

## What happened to my mother?

This story was written for *you*. It was written to open *your* eyes to the reality of what is going on day after day – even in good hospitals with excellent reputations.

Where this occurred is not important because it can happen anywhere.

### The doctor visit – May 21

Mother was looking forward to her appointment with an orthopedist to discuss her knee pain. I happened to be in town for a visit. My sister and I joined Mother and listened as she told the doctor how the cortisone shots had not helped and admitted just how much pain she was in. She had a very high threshold for pain so we knew it must be bad. Mother described the impact this was having on her: it was difficult and painful to stand from a seated position, she was not able to walk for long distances, and getting in and out of the car was challenging. Driving (this was her right knee) was becoming more painful. The orthopedist looked at her x-rays and confirmed that knee replacement was warranted but offered that she could continue with cortisone shots and pain relievers. He left the room to give us time to talk. I was most concerned about the risk of Mother falling. She lived with my sister, Jeanne, who had noticed how she was staying home more and was less inclined to get together with her friends from church. Surgery was clearly the favored option for all three of us – to relieve Mother's pain and allow her to resume her activities.

Since she was under the care of three physicians (primary care – who had referred her for the consult; cardiologist; and endocrinologist), the orthopedist insisted on written releases clearing her for surgery. He gave forms to Mother for each physician to sign. Before leaving the office, his staff scheduled an MRI to aid in the design of the knee prosthetic in preparation for surgery set for August 24.

Mother insisted that before going home, she be driven to the physicians' offices to drop off the releases. She could not wait to get this underway knowing she would soon get pain relief – just as she had experienced with her other knee replacement surgery ten years ago.

I flew back home knowing I would see Mother in September to be with her the first week home from rehab. The orthopedist and his assistant fully described the expected recovery time line so I knew when to request vacation when I returned to work. The decline in Mother's health made leaving difficult.

## July

Her primary care physician and the endocrinologist had signed the releases for Mother's surgery, but the cardiologist insisted that she have a stress test. I wasn't sure how well I would do if I had a stress test, so I certainly wondered about Mother's ability at 81 years old. Based on the results of that stress test, the cardiologist scheduled her for a cardiac catheterization. My sister, Jeanne, was scheduled to be out of town for a conference when this procedure was added on July 5th. Her friend, Fran, fortunately a nurse, offered to take Mother. As soon as Jeanne returned, another procedure was scheduled at the hospital to insert a heart stent the following week on July 13th. Hearing about all this from hundreds of miles away, I couldn't understand why they weren't taking Mother immediately from one procedure to another rather than having her endure all these delays in scheduling. Then I learned that the procedures were done at different locations.

Mother developed problems in her groin, the site of the cardiac cath entry, and returned to the cardiologist who scheduled more tests on July 25th. Those tests revealed peripheral artery disease. The cardiologist wanted to insert stents in Mother's legs. Her primary care physician intervened and requested that further tests and procedures be delayed until after the knee replacement surgery as that was the primary need at the time.

## August

The cardiologist complied, signed off, and Mother was cleared for knee surgery – a full four months after her initial orthopedic visit. Surgery was scheduled for September 21, a month later than originally planned.

Hearing the news, I quickly searched healthcare quality internet sites to look up the hospital's ratings. I was pleased to see the high rankings comparing that hospital favorably to the national averages and to hospitals with which I was more familiar.

Mother was actually looking forward to knee surgery – for pain relief. She diligently followed the surgery prep instructions that included discontinuing her Coumadin (blood thinner). Jeanne was great about keeping me informed every step of the way.

## Surgery – September 21

The surgery was considered a success but it was unclear how long Mother would remain in the hospital since they wanted to carefully manage her blood levels to avoid clotting. She had suffered a stroke in 1983 when she was only 54 and had been on Coumadin ever since.

Everything went well. Mother was discharged right on schedule, five days after surgery, to a rehab facility for an expected two-week stay. She was transported by ambulance to the facility.

## Rehab facility – September 26

I smiled when Jeanne suggested I call Mother on her cell phone. I had given the phone to her a couple of years before for safety reasons. She mostly kept it plugged in for charging and hardly ever used it. When the monthly bills came, I was so hopeful that she would use it even for just a minute or two. Her voice was strong when she spoke with me. "I'll be home in two weeks!" She sounded excited to see me.

All the updates I got from Jeanne were quite positive about Mother's rehab sessions and continued improvement. The only thing that was concerning was a sore (a pressure ulcer) developing on her left heel, which fortunately was not the same leg as the knee surgery. As a result of the stroke, she had no sensory perception on her left side so she could not feel the wound, which got worse as she scooted herself around in bed. It was discovered by the wound nurse in rehab and no one could be sure if she had it when she arrived or if it started at that facility.

Mother pushed herself to go to the rehab gym every day as scheduled and did all her exercises in bed as instructed. She used a walker to go short distances though she still needed someone to walk behind her since she didn't quite have her strength back. She knew I was scheduled to fly in on Saturday, October 9th, the day she was expected to be discharged. Mother insisted she go home as planned, two weeks after surgery.

## Going home – October 9

Jeanne got Mother home on Saturday morning, and had the housekeeper's daughter (who had recently completed her certification as a nursing assistant) stay with her while Jeanne picked me up at the airport.

It was such a relief to see Mother doing well and I was glad I could give Jeanne a break since she had missed some work and spent part of every day at the hospital or rehab facility.

The doctor ordered home care services for Mother, which was a relief since she was still quite weak. A nurse met with all three of us to let us know what to expect. She evaluated Mother, took photos and measurements of the sore on her heel that was getting deeper, then showed us how to change the dressing every day. She expressed concern about the wound.

I ran errands while the home care staff worked with Mother. The physical therapist recommended a special lift chair to replace Mother's old recliner to make it easier for her to get up and down. I went to a medical supply store to try out the different sizes and borrowed fabric samples so Jeanne and Mother could make the selection. When I got home, I was surprised to see Mother on a seat in the bath tub, wound exposed and soaking in the bath water. The occupational therapist with her assured me it was okay.

The home care company monitored Mother's vital signs every day with equipment connected to the telephone line. They showed us how to assist Mother at the same time each morning with weight, blood pressure, and pulse oximetry for nurses in the office to assess.

Mother was diligent with her strengthening exercises and walking around the house with the walker (with someone close behind). However, she was clearly too weak to be left home alone after the first week was over and I had to fly back. Jeanne and I started calling a list of recommended sitters and agencies, pleased to learn that the woman who had taken care of our uncle a couple of years earlier was available and happy to be a companion for Mother, to assist with meals and errands, if needed, while Jeanne worked. With me scheduled to leave in just a couple of days, we decided to also meet with an agency and register with them in the event a back-up sitter was needed.

Late the very next day the woman we were counting on called back to say that she needed to find full-time work and wouldn't be able to help after all. In a panic, I quickly called the agency. It was just after 5:00 p.m. (on Friday) and I wanted to request a sitter for Monday. The phone rang and rang and rang without anyone answering – without even a voice messaging system answering. Clearly, I had to have misdialed. I looked back in the packet left by the agency to find another piece of paper with the phone number on it and compared it to the business card I had just used to place the call. The numbers were the same and both referenced that it was answered twenty-four hours a day. So it was obvious that I had misdialed.

After repeated attempts, no one ever answered the phone at the agency.

In the meantime, Jeanne had called her housekeeper's daughter (the CNA) and she had some limited availability and agreed to come the next morning to learn about the telemonitoring equipment and stay with Mother while Jeanne took me to the airport.

## October 16

During the first leg of my flight home, I could not shake the uneasy feeling that I must return to take care of my mother. As I landed at the airport, where I had a two-hour layover, my mind was racing to figure things out. I was upset that I had even gotten on the plane in the first place. I called my sister to talk about what to do next. Jeanne answered her cell phone full of excitement that Teresa, a long-time family friend, could come the next day to help out with Mother. We both cried with such relief. I could continue my trip home knowing my mother would be well cared for by Teresa.

Later that night, Jeanne sent me a text with a photo of Mother. Jeanne had used the curling iron on Mother's hair to style the haircut I gave her before I left.

Jeanne and I felt comforted knowing that Mother would be in good, trusted hands.

## Back to the hospital – October 17

I was stunned by what Jeanne told me on the phone the very next day when our friend, Teresa, was to arrive. "Mother screamed saying she was in excruciating pain in her knee and she couldn't walk." Something was terribly wrong because Mother had such a high tolerance for pain and rarely complained. Jeanne called the home care agency and spoke with the nurse who had assessed the telemonitoring that morning and reviewed the vital trends: her blood pressure was up and her weight had been going up so she must be retaining fluid. The nurse recommended that she be taken to the emergency department.

Mother was taken to the hospital by ambulance (just three weeks after being discharged). After hours of waiting, it was determined that she had an infection in her knee and would require a second surgery to reopen and clean the prosthesis.

## October 23

Teresa stayed with Mother each day in the hospital so Jeanne could continue to work. Teresa updated Jeanne when she arrived. Then my sister updated me. The surgery seemed to go okay, but Mother would have to start the rehab routine all over again.

Mother was transferred to the rehab facility after five days in the hospital, just like the first time. It was such a relief to know that Teresa was going to be with her there as well.

## Back to rehab – October 28

Staff at the rehab facility welcomed Mother back for another two-week stay. They had genuinely enjoyed Mother's pleasant attitude, sense of humor, and determination to follow the rehab regimen. She needed a lot more attention this time with the reopened incision and the pressure ulcer on her heel, which was much deeper than when she was there two weeks before. When Jeanne arrived each evening, it seemed there were more questions than answers about Mother's care. Teresa was too shy to talk to the caregivers, but she would tell Jeanne all about how each day progressed with complaints about what occurred. Jeanne then approached the staff with concerns about what she had heard and pushed for plans about next steps.

Mother was transported by ambulance for a follow-up visit with the infectious disease specialist. She was on the gurney for at least four hours – from the rehab facility to the doctor's waiting room to the exam room.

After a few more days, Teresa's family called to ask when she would be home. The plan had been for Teresa to assist Mother at home. But the situation had changed. Teresa left. She could possibly return after Mother went home.

It was hard to imagine Mother spending all that time at the rehab facility alone. Even though Teresa wasn't assertive with the nursing staff about Mother's needs, she kept Mother company and was another pair of eyes to keep Jeanne informed. I scheduled another week off work to coincide with Mother's expected return home.

Jeanne asked friends to sit with Mother at the rehab facility for a couple of hours during the day. Jeanne also started missing a lot of work again to be there herself. Mother did not progress as expected and missed some of the treatment sessions with the physical therapist. She developed a fever and congestion, her pressure ulcer continued to worsen, and her knee began to drain at the incision site. She was sent back to the infectious disease specialist.

After just one week at the rehab facility, Mother couldn't pass urine and was clearly distressed. She was transported back to the emergency department on Monday, November 1st with suspected renal failure.

## Back for the third time – November 1

I was so anxious to get my daily calls from Jeanne. Hearing Mother was taken back to the emergency department made me realize how serious the situation was becoming. Mother stayed on a gurney in the ED hallway for hours – no rooms available. I was furious. Why the hell didn't they just admit her since she was so sick? I had to be careful not to express my anger and instead sound reassuring and supportive on the phone with my sister.

Jeanne described the situation. "When our three aunts arrived only one person could visit at a time. Mother was right out in the corridor. We took turns with her, but our aunts started leaving since it was taking so long. Finally a space opened up where Mother could be catheterized for the urine build up." Jeanne stayed by Mother's side while many tests were performed throughout the night.

At 3 a.m., after eight hours in emergency, Mother was finally admitted to an isolation room on the cardiac unit with the diagnoses of congestive heart failure and MRSA – her kidneys were fine. It was inconceivable that after spending all that time center stage in the corridor of the ED, that you couldn't be in her room now without wearing protective gown and gloves.

Mother's primary care physician of fourteen years was on rotation at the hospital for the first three days and began talking with Mother about the gravity of her condition. A consulting cardiologist and the same infectious disease physician were involved with Mother's case. She was also visited by her orthopedic surgeon apologizing that all this had happened to her. He carefully explained that the only way to get rid of the infection was to have surgery again to remove the prosthetic – the MRSA was sticking to it. She would not be able to walk without it. After six weeks, yet another surgery would be necessary to put the knee prosthesis back in. The cardiologist, however, informed us that an echocardiogram indicated her heart had weakened and was functioning at a diminished capacity. A cardiac event had occurred, perhaps during her last surgery. The stent might not be functioning as intended. He said they could explore the condition of her heart with surgery but he would consider that a high risk. She could have the prosthesis removed, but that was a high risk due to her heart. She could do nothing, but that was a high risk due to the infection. It was the cardiologist's opinion, supported by her primary care physician, that Mother's heart would fail if she underwent surgery again – and she would die on the operating table.

## November 4

Jeanne's voice was getting shakier every time I spoke to her. The days seemed very long as I waited for my flight to go back there on Saturday. I went ahead and packed up everything except my toiletries on Thursday night. Now perhaps I could enjoy dinner out with my husband, Jim, after work.

## November 5

Around 8 a.m. my sister called me at work to let me know that Mother's primary care physician wanted to have a family conference with all three of us that morning. At 9 a.m. they called me – the physician, Jeanne, and Mother all on speaker phone in Mother's room. The doctor spoke directly to Mother while we listened. At that moment, I was thankful I was not in that room. I could not control my tears. When the doctor finished her matter-of-fact speech about how dire things were, she asked if we had any questions. The call ended and I slowly went back to my desk. Jeanne called me back. "Can you come today and not wait until tomorrow?"

I called Jim to see what he could do to get me on a flight right away. I left work immediately, at 9:30 a.m., and drove the nineteen miles home as fast as I could safely maneuver. Jim had printed my boarding pass and put my suitcase in the car (thank God, I packed early!). He laid out my toiletries all over the dining room table for me to select what I needed and throw it in a bag. At 10:15 a.m. we headed to the airport ten miles away. Jim drove even faster than I had. I still shake my head wondering how we got me on that plane in time for departure at 11:30 a.m.

## Family reunion

I was supposed to be returning to help Mother with her rehab. Instead, I found myself calling my daughter and son to come see their Gramma before it was too late. She was incredibly weak, unable to swallow much of anything without choking, and I wanted them to get there quickly so she would still recognize them.

I didn't get to meet Mother's primary care physician because her rotation was up. Her partner from the clinic had taken over Mother's case.

The next day, I watched as a nurse gave Mother a shot in her stomach and when I asked if that was Heparin, the nurse nodded affirmatively. Later, I asked the covering physician why Mother was on two blood thinners: Heparin and Coumadin. The response was as expected. "She doesn't need to be on both." I watched the same nurse the next time she gave the meds and approached her to assure myself that she was no longer going to give Mother a Heparin shot. I asked to see her in the hall, because I didn't want anyone to overhear – but the nurse already knew what I was going to say. With a sheepish look she said, "It was discontinued." A few days later, I noticed that the urine in the catheter bag wasn't dark red anymore and Mother had stopped spitting up blood.

Mother had a hard time swallowing and had to be suctioned frequently so her doctor ordered soft foods for her. She later experienced pain when drinking or eating anything cold. We requested that the doctor change the dietary order from soft food to whatever Mother could tolerate. The next morning, someone from Nutrition Services came to the room to talk with Mother about menu selections. Jeanne and I were pleased with the attention and the food choices. We selected the menu for her next three meals – from the offerings provided by the dietician.

The same person returned each morning to ask about meal selections. Each time the meal tray was brought, it did not contain any of the food or beverage that Mother ordered. And, each time the nurses on the cardiac unit offered to make soup and decaf coffee for her. Puzzled, we asked repeatedly why the food requested was never what was brought to the room. The Nutrition Services staff said they would check on it. The nurses on the cardiac unit said they would check on it. The doctor said she had changed the dietary order.

Mother had to start taking her medications with decaf coffee, needing the warmth to soothe the pain. She was so frustrated with eating the same soup and decaf coffee over and over again. Why did they bother to take her order if they weren't going to listen to what she asked for? Everyone always acted surprised that she didn't get what she ordered.

After Mother had been on the cardiac unit for five days, the nurse manager stopped by to see her and ask if things were going okay with her stay on the Unit. Jeanne and I expressed our frustration with meals. He sounded so surprised and said he would check on that right away. Mother was on the Unit for another four days. We never saw the nurse manager again.

Finally, the Nutrition Services staff explained that the doctor's changed order was never communicated to them so they had to continue to follow the original soft food order even though Mother's tray was continually returned untouched.

*****

## November 7

My daughter and son flew in and made the most of their twenty-four-hour trip, wearing protective gowns and gloves, but reminiscing and playing games. Mother perked up and insisted on keeping her mind sharp – plus she loved winning. She held court in her hospital room with frequent visitors who all had to don the yellow gowns. No one could fathom that this woman who embodied *Live, Laugh, Love* was going to slip away from them.

After the brief family reunion, the hard decisions remained. The orthopedic surgeon was eager to get Mother's heart stabilized for surgery the next week. He had contacted a colleague who had been doing less invasive procedures and was willing to consult on Mother's case. Since the antibiotics had not helped, the only other option to get rid of the MRSA was to amputate. I told him that we were confused because the cardiologist told us that she would likely die on the operating table because her heart was too weak to withstand another surgery. I asked him to please talk to the cardiologist directly before we got our hopes up.

Just a couple of hours later, Jeanne and I headed to the hospital cafeteria. The orthopedist walked off the elevator and seemed glad to see us. Standing by the open elevator, he said he was sorry – but surgery was definitely not recommended. We wondered when he might have told us if we hadn't bumped into him. We never saw him again.

## Decisions

Mother told all of us that she would make a decision on Monday, November 8th, after considering the options given to her:

1   *Surgery for the third time to remove the knee prosthesis to fully rid the MRSA followed by a fourth surgery six weeks later to replace the prosthesis. She would most likely die on the operating table.*
2   *Amputation. That would still require surgery . . . with the same terminal outcome. So how was that any different?*
3   *Do nothing. The hospice director invited Mother to spend her final days in the beautiful, peaceful Hospice Care Center (where they accept patients for palliative care who are expected to die within six weeks).*
4   *Do nothing. Go home. The hospice director described how Mother's bedroom could be converted with a hospital bed, oxygen, suction, and medical supplies so hospice care could be provided at home to keep her comfortable.*

## November 8

On Monday afternoon, after my adult children returned to their respective homes, Mother made her decision: "No heroics." She wanted to go home with hospice care. Jeanne and I could not reconcile that the beautiful Hospice Care Center (we knew it well because we had walked the outdoor labyrinth there) was even an option since admission was based on anticipated death within six weeks. Everything went quickly into motion to get all the arrangements made for her to be taken home by ambulance on Wednesday.

My sister and I knew we could be nowhere other than by our Mother's side. Jeanne called the school where she worked to talk about reducing hours, working from home, and only going to the office to do payroll or other absolutely critical onsite work. I called my husband about needing to stay with Mother and really having no clue when I would fly home. He supported me by saying: "Do what you have to do." Then I called my employer about FMLA (Family Medical Leave Act). We agreed to a half-time arrangement since I was able to connect to the office remotely.

Jeanne and I had a lot to do before Mother was discharged from the hospital. Neighbors helped rearrange Mother's bedroom to make room for the hospital bed, oxygen, and suction equipment. We removed all of her clothes from the closet except for the new gowns and bed jackets and placed the chest of drawers in the closet. That became the medical supply closet nicely hidden behind the folding doors. The long dresser was moved to the opposite wall so that the hospital bed could be placed to give Mother the optimum view through the wall of windows. They took apart her sleep number bed and stored it in the boxes supplied by the local store.

When the neighbors left, we looked at the stark room and thought about Mother being in there. Right away we noticed the mirror on the dresser that had to go so she couldn't see herself. Then Jeanne had a great idea – she took the colorful quilted shams they had just removed from Mother's bed and hung them over the dresser. We stapled the get-well cards she got in the hospital onto the shams. On the seven-foot-long dresser, we arranged flowers and family photographs from around the house. It started to look a little more welcoming. The next morning, the hospital bed and medical equipment were delivered and we were given instructions on their use. We got the bed made with flowered sheets adding the finishing touches with folding guest chairs. The room was as ready as it could be for Mother's arrival that afternoon.

## Returning home – November 10

Mother was brought home by ambulance. Jeanne and I had no idea how she would react to a homecoming in this unexpected condition. We were greeted with Mother's laughter as she chatted with the EMTs who remembered transporting her before. As they wheeled her stretcher in, Mother talked about all the changes to her room and was clearly glad to be home. So much had happened to her since she left home twenty-four days ago. It finally hit me that she hadn't been home since I was there – she had been taken to the hospital the day after I left in October. She returned home never to walk again – never to leave her bedroom.

*****

The first two weeks at home were quite lively. Mother held court while friends, neighbors, family all came to spend time with her. Musicians from church came to serenade her and had even written a song about her. A family friend, a well-known professional musician, came to visit and played the piano from the nearby living room for her to hear.

Mother still wanted to do crossword puzzles and play games. Jeanne and I, as well as visitors, had a great time laughing with her and enjoying her company.

Mother came to love the sound of the squeaky brakes on the mail delivery truck. The highlight of each day was the stack of cards from all over the country from family and friends sending greetings and love. One friend, who couldn't get out to visit (or more likely just couldn't handle the reality of Mother's situation) sent a card every single day.

Mother was known for mailing over two hundred birthday cards each year with personal notes and decorative stickers. She needed help with the December birthdays so she gave me instructions on where to find the big box of cards, stamps, stickers, birthday date book, and address book. I was directed to write a list of names and specific dates for the December cards then address the envelopes. Mother selected a card for each person, signed them, then personalized them with stickers. In the dining room on the sideboard were the remaining November cards to be mailed, and she gave strict orders not to mail them out too soon. Once the December cards were ready, I placed them in date order on the sideboard. One day in mid-December, I just couldn't stand the thought of someone receiving a card after Mother died, so I mailed all the remaining cards even though I knew she wouldn't be happy.

Mother asked us to start bringing her papers from the filing cabinet, boxes, and desk drawer contents to her bed. She went through everything over a few days: threw things away, put papers in recycling, and had us bundle up materials and photographs to give (or mail) to certain people. Memories filled the room as my sister and I took turns being with Mother sifting through her past.

## The final days

With Mother being so alert, laughing, and enjoying her visitors, Jeanne and I began to question if hospice care was really the best that could be done. Maybe she could handle surgery. Perhaps there were specialists that could help. Why had we complied with Mother's request to simply do nothing and go home? I called the hospice care office to schedule an appointment with the counselor since Mother seemed to be getting better.

My sister and I cried with anger, frustration, and sadness hearing the counselor describe our Mother as rallying a bit since she was in her own bedroom and making her own choices about her final days. The counselor clearly stated that Mother would not get better because the MRSA would not go away.

We were on a roller coaster ride – one day Mother seemed like she was on the road to recovery wanting to play games and eating at least a few bites at all three meal times. The next day she was weak, confused, and sleeping most of the time. Her heel improved. Her knee was bendable 90 degrees but the wound color kept changing – red, then clear, then brownish. Her heart was becoming weaker and every effort exhausted her. I wondered how much time we had left with her . . . how could we make her comfortable . . . were we hurting her or helping her? Nothing stayed consistent from day to day.

*****

All the visitors to the home were compliant and discreet about following the precautions required and posted:

*NO SMOKING, OXYGEN IN USE posted on the front door*
*DON'T FORGET TO WASH YOUR HANDS WHEN LEAVING posted in the foyer and just outside Mother's bedroom*

For those who had any cuts whatsoever on their hands or who just wanted extra protection, there was a box of gloves just inside the bedroom. The visitors' path of travel couldn't be better: enter the front door, turn left into a hallway and left again into Mother's bedroom; then leave her bedroom and take the first left into the bathroom to wash hands with special soap and dry hands with paper towels; then around the corner back out the front door. As visitors left, she reminded them to wash their hands.

Jeanne bought Mother such pretty night gowns and pajamas, using the tops as bed jackets. I cut her hair very short, which looked great with all the weight she had lost.

What Mother could view from her bed became of utmost importance. Fortunately, windows filled almost the entire wall to her right. She insisted the head of her bed and her pillows be adjusted so she could look out the window to view a yard full of trees, squirrels running around, birds at a feeder, and the activity of cars in the driveway and people walking to the front door.

Facing forward, she dubbed the view on the wall and dresser as her "eye candy." To her left, were chairs available for her numerous visitors. Padded folding chairs worked well and could be easily stored behind the door to convert the room from a social gathering space back to a patient care room for baths and nurse visits.

What Mother saw seemed to give her comfort and excitement, anticipation with approaching visitors, as well as a sense of control. She directed where she wanted new cards and photographs placed for her maximum viewing pleasure and to feel a connection with others.

As time passed, the room became a place of solace with good-byes and last rites.

*****

## November 23

My husband flew in two days before Thanksgiving and visited with Mother as soon as he arrived. The very next day, the priest and all the local family were called to say their good-byes as it seemed that death was imminent. My son returned for his annual Thanksgiving visit. It was fortunate that he had traveled to see Mother three weeks earlier since she had started declining rapidly. We were shocked by the sudden change in our Mother's condition. We took turns sleeping on the floor by her side the next few nights.

Mother had spent a lot of time over the prior week planning details of her own memorial service: the music to be played, the songs for all to sing, and the specific Bible verses – she went through her different Bibles in search of the exact wording she remembered – because it had to be all about love.

Even from her death bed, she continued to teach us. This time the lessons were: (1) the only thing that matters in life is love, and (2) if you plan your own funeral, you can still have the last word.

*****

Mother started planning a party and told us who to invite. The list became very long – over forty people. She even specified when it should be – on Saturday, December 11th, from 1:00–5:00. Jeanne and I just could not bear the thought of a house full of people and struggled with what to do since we wanted to fulfill all her requests. We asked the hospice counselor to talk with Mother. When she was asked why she wanted a party, she explained that she wanted to "thank everyone."

*****

Jeanne and I both had such a hard time getting work done but we had to keep at it so we could put in the hours to get our paychecks and benefits. We took turns retreating to the sunroom to work on our laptops. We had interviewed a sitter to be with Mother while we both worked, but it just did not feel right bringing a stranger into Mother's room when there were so many family and friends who wanted to be with her.

It was hard to leave the house for any length of time worrying that she might take her last breath without one or both of us by her side. We took turns grabbing a few items from the grocery store. Jeanne went to work briefly once each week. I simply had to get fresh air and take walks some days. I really enjoyed escaping with a neighbor to a sports bar to watch the familiar Green Bay Packers. My husband mailed my football jersey to me which put a big smile on my face.

Somehow it was obvious which roles each of us should take on as we became caregivers around the clock. Jeanne assisted with bathing and bed pans, working with the nurse and nursing assistant to clean and wrap the worsening pressure ulcer and the changing surgical site that drained at times, and was obviously turning a darker tone all around the knee. She emptied out the catheter bag and kept a privacy cloth where it was attached to the bed. Jeanne did a great job assuring Mother's dignity as her bodily functions declined.

I assumed responsibility for medications: a lot to manage with the multitude of pills several times a day that continually changed as her condition deteriorated. Several medications were discontinued; and when she could no longer swallow pills, liquids were ordered. After not eating for five days, she didn't have the strength to even suck on a straw so the liquids had to be slowly squirted in her mouth. The hospice team was emphatic about Mother getting her meds around the clock to alleviate pain so we took turns setting alarms throughout the night. It was hard to comprehend why we would wake Mother up during the night to give her pain meds when she was sleeping soundly. The hospice nurse explained that she needed to keep the meds in her system or the pain would build up and be more difficult to control.

One of my shifts did not go well after giving Mother some thick pink pain medication – she promptly started spitting it up and had to be suctioned. After careful review the next day with the hospice team, they all agreed that palliative care was the only goal at this stage so all medications were discontinued except the morphine and something to keep the fluid down so she wouldn't have to be suctioned.

Mother's last meal was ice cream . . . her very favorite food.

## The end – December 20

Jeanne and I woke up agitated that Mother was so weak and it was heartbreaking to watch her linger. I called the hospice team to come talk to us because we were both very upset – it seemed so unfair. She had gone twelve days without food and four days without water. We needed to know what would happen next.

"It's time!" my sister called out to me. It was about 9:30 p.m. I had taken a shower and was putting on my pajamas and just heard the alarm go off for Mother's morphine dose. I thought Jeanne was being impatient and responded, "I'll be right there." I hurried downstairs and started to open the refrigerator to grab the morphine when she said again: "No, it's time." I was stunned to hear those words. I couldn't believe I had any more tears left. We walked together to her room and Jeanne softly shared that her breathing was different. We sat on each side of our Mother until her last breath two hours later. The finality of that last breath was still surprising. Isn't that what we had been preparing for?

Six weeks – just like the hospice director said.

## What happened to my mother?

Seven months. Seven months on a roller coaster ride – with hopes for a better, pain-free life for Mother that turned downhill ending her life instead (see Time Line, Figure 1.1).

With the shift to value-based reimbursement tied to patient outcomes, patient satisfaction, and cost – this experience rated poorly. It was everything but coordinated care. Though Mother's case entailed four of the Partnership for Patients areas of focus (see Table 1.1), only one – severe pressure ulcer – is on Medicare's list for non-payment for "increased costs of care that result when a patient is harmed" (Centers for Medicare & Medicaid).

Healthcare costs across the nation vary drastically, but I don't think anyone anywhere can disagree with me that $52,409 is a lot to spend just on pre-op services. This alarming amount raises many questions – unfortunately for my mother, retrospectively.

*Why did no one notice the accumulation of these charges as unusual?*
*Why did no one question if moving forward with surgery was still a good idea?*
*Why was the risk of surgery not revisited after all the time spent for pre-op services?*
*With electronic health records, why can't unusually high charges trigger notification?*
*Who was watching?*
*Who was coordinating?*
No one.

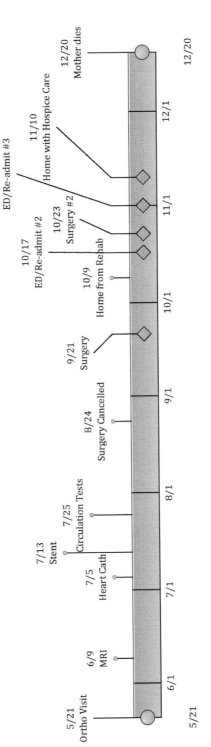

*Figure 1.1* Case study time line: what happened to my mother?

*Table 1.1* Case study preventable harm

| Preventable Incident | Mother's Case |
|---|---|
| Pressure Ulcer | Left heel |
| Medication Error | Two blood thinners |
| Surgical Infection | Knee replacement – MRSA |
| Readmissions | Three total admissions within seven weeks |

## Why is this important?

For Medicare patients, the U.S. average charges for total knee replacement totaled $60,500: $1,900 for pre-surgical preparation, $56,000 for hospital stay and surgery, plus $2,600 for post-surgical care, according to a *Healthline* article, "Understanding Knee Replacement Costs: What's on the Bill?" (Greengard 2012).

Some improvement has been made nationally in reducing patient harm as reported in "Efforts to Improve Patient Safety Result in 1.3 Million Fewer Patient Harms" (AHRQ 2013). But you **must** understand the context of the improvement as later reported: in 2010 the ratio was 145 harms per 1,000 discharges; the 2013 reported improvement was 121 harms per 1,000 discharges (AHRQ 2015). The Partnership for Patients program led by CMS is doing great work to reduce preventable harm and they must not slow down because there is so far to go.

Get on board and find the best fit for your organization to join in the improvement efforts. Consider Partnership for Patients, Institute for Healthcare Improvement (IHI), ThedaCare Center for Healthcare Value, Agency for Healthcare Research and Quality (AHRQ).

## Epilogue

There were so many people involved in caring for Mother, my sister, and me. Without the support of so many who offered their time, their helping hands and strong arms, their preparation of meals, their phone calls, their visits, their cards, their music, their prayers, their hugs and kind words – there is no way that Jeanne and I could have managed to care for Mother at home, where she wanted to spend her final days.

Acknowledgements and thanks cannot convey the importance of that support. Jeanne and I hope that the telling of this story will demonstrate what a difference every encounter made.

Special recognition goes to my husband who took my phone call with such compassion when I couldn't come home, didn't know when I could, and would have to take a leave from work. We had never been apart that long since the day we met and now we were more than 1,000 miles from each other. He called me at least twice every day.

My son and daughter quickly responded to my call to be with their Gramma in the hospital. They did not just show up. They entertained her with photographs, stories, and games. The stuffed animal they gave Mother as they said good-bye was showcased to all visitors from that day on.

Jeanne and I were blessed to have three aunts and a cousin in town to sit with Mother on occasion. These generous women, Mother's sisters-in-law, bought groceries and planned and served meals for gatherings.

I came to understand the real meaning of community by experiencing the many relationships that Mother and Jeanne had built as very active members in their church, in their neighborhood, and even in Jeanne's place of work. It seemed that we never had to ask for help because someone was always there to offer first.

It was truly a community who helped Mother make the most of her last six weeks of life.

Thank you.

## Bibliography

Agency for Healthcare Research and Quality (AHRQ). 2013 Interim Report. "Efforts to Improve Patient Safety Result in 1.3 Million Fewer Patient Harms." Accessed August 7, 2016. http://www.ahrq.gov/professionals/quality-patient-safety/pfp/interimhacrate2013.html

Agency for Healthcare Research and Quality (AHRQ). October 2015. "2013 Annual Hospital-Acquired Condition Rate and Estimates of Cost Savings and Deaths Averted from 2010–2013." *AHRQ Publication No. 16–0006-EF*. Accessed August 7, 2016. http://www.ahrq.gov/professionals/qualitypatient-safety/pfp/index.html

Centers for Medicare & Medicaid Services (CMS). "Patient Safety Areas of Focus." Accessed August 7, 2016. https://partnershipforpatients.cms.gov/about-the-partnership/what-is-the-partnership-about/lpwhat-the-partnership-is-about.html

Greengard, Samuel. 2012. Medically Reviewed by George Krucik, MD, MBA. Updated February 23, 2015. "Understanding Knee Replacement Costs: What's on the Bill?" *Healthline*. Accessed August 7, 2016. http://www.healthline.com/health/total-knee-replacement-surgery/understanding-costs

# 2 Discussion topics

## What was the impact?

### Introduction

Probing questions about the case study encourage open discussion with your team about the impact of un-coordinated care and preventable harm on patients, their extended families, and communities, and the cost created by harm.

Recommended research topics are included for consideration based on your organization's learning needs.

### Discussion: physician visits

There were so many physicians involved in Mother's care and the following briefly identifies them and their relationship to her as a patient.

### What happened?

#### Physician office visits before surgery

- Mother was referred to an **orthopedic specialist** for knee pain that had not been resolved with cortisone injections. She met with the specialist who recommended knee replacement surgery. Since Mother was under the care of several other specialists plus her primary care physician, the orthopedist wanted a written release from the other physicians stating that she was cleared for knee surgery. Mother was handed the forms to take to each physician for sign-off.
- Her **cardiologist** would not sign the release for surgery without a stress test. After the stress test, the cardiologist scheduled a cardiac catheterization. He then scheduled a procedure for the following week to insert a stent. Mother developed leg pain and severe bruising in the groin area and returned to the cardiologist who then scheduled further tests with concern for circulation in her legs.
- After those tests, with no indication of blood clots in her legs, her **primary care physician** intervened and requested that any further tests be delayed until after knee replacement surgery, to eliminate the debilitating pain, as that was the primary need at the time.

- The **cardiologist** signed off and Mother was cleared for knee replacement surgery – a full four months after the initial orthopedic visit.
- The **orthopedic specialist** ordered an MRI for selection of the knee prosthetic.

## Physician visits after surgery

- Mother was visited by her **primary care physician** in the hospital after her knee replacement surgery. They discussed her options for a rehab facility after discharge.

## Physician visits during third admission

- When Mother was admitted to the same hospital for the third time, her **primary care physician** was the attending and was on rotation for the first three days of the hospitalization. After that, a partner from the office took over Mother's case.
- When Mother was discharged from the hospital to her home with hospice care, her primary care physician visited her twice after office hours and was updated on her case by the **hospice physician**.
- Mother died six weeks after being discharged from the hospital.

## Discussion

1 Discuss how the physicians and all other parties involved followed, or failed to follow, the Partnership for Patients description.

> "Safe, effective, and efficient care transitions require thoughtful collaboration among health care providers, hospitals, nursing homes and other facilities, social service providers, patient caregivers, and patients themselves."
> (CMS, "Community-Based Care Transitions Program")

2 The orthopedic surgeon gave Mother the release forms for her physicians to sign for surgery clearance. The cardiologist did not sign off until the primary care physician requested he hold off on further tests until after the knee surgery. What was the communication chain and what impact did that have on Mother?

3 The only family conference held was with the primary care physician and not until November 5. Should other physicians have participated? Each physician spoke independently to the family. What was the impact on the family?

4 There were many physicians involved in Mother's care:

- Primary care physician
- Primary care physician's clinic partner during hospital rotation
- Orthopedic surgeon
- Cardiologist during pre-op
- Consulting cardiologist during the third admission
- Infectious disease specialist during the second rehab stay and during the third admission

- Rehab facility physician
- Hospitalist

What interactions did these physicians have? What communication should be expected between them?

## Recommended research topics

- Team-Based Care at Mayo Clinic:

  McCarthy, Douglas, Kimberly Mueller, and Jennifer Wrenn. August 2009. "Mayo Clinic: Multidisciplinary Teamwork, Physician-Led Governance, and Patient-Centered Culture Drive World-Class Health Care." *The Commonwealth Fund*, pub 1306, Vol. 27. Accessed August 9, 2016. http://www.commonwealthfund.org/~/media/Files/Publications/Case%20Study/2009/Aug/1306_McCarthy_Mayo_case%20study.pdf

- Partnership for Patients:

  https://partnershipforpatients.cms.gov

## Discussion: inpatient

1   As a family member, what if I had not noticed (or did not know enough to speak up) about the double dose of blood thinners? Who was supposed to reconcile the medications? Pharmacy? Attending physician? Nurse? Who?
2   Talk about the communication between physicians and how that should occur?

   a   Should there have been an interdisciplinary care conference?
   b   What was the impact of each physician speaking separately to Mother and her two daughters?

3   Where did the pressure ulcer come from? The hospital? Rehab? Who was responsible for noticing the beginning of the skin breakdown?

## Recommended research topics

- Agency for Healthcare Research and Quality (AHRQ):

  www.ahrq.gov

- Joint Commission National Patient Safety Goals:

  http://www.jointcommission.org/standards_information/npsgs.aspx

- Patient and Family Centered Care Organizational Self-Assessment Tool:

  Institute for Healthcare Improvement and National Institute for Children's Health Quality, developed in partnership with the Institute for Patient- and Family-Centered Care. June 2013. "Patient- and Family-Centered Care Organizational Self-Assessment Tool." Accessed August 7, 2016. http://www.ihi.org/resources/Pages/Tools/PatientFamilyCenteredCareOrganizationalSelfAssessmentTool.aspx

- Transforming Care at the Bedside:

  Lee, B., D. Shannon, P. Rutherford, and C. Peck. 2008. *Transforming Care at the Bedside How-to Guide: Optimizing Communication and Teamwork.* Cambridge, MA: Institute for Healthcare Improvement. Accessed August 10, 2016. www.ihi.org

### Discussion: surgery

1  Talk about the role that my sister and I played in Mother's care. If Mother had not had such involved family, what do you think might have happened differently?

   a  What could my sister and I have done to improve the outcome?
   b  What type of service agencies could have been utilized to assist Mother?

2  Describe the communication and coordination physician to physician concerning Mother's care.

   a  What is the family's role in having physicians talk to each other about the risk of surgery?
   b  How could this situation have been better served by a team approach?

3  Was surgery the best option for this 81-year-old in the first place?

   a  How might a second opinion been warranted, and at what stage?
   b  Who would be responsible for insisting on or recommending a second opinion?

4  The Institute for Healthcare Improvement (IHI) launched the Project JOINTS initiative in April 2011 and reported in "Preventing Infection After Hip and Knee Replacements:"

   > "Knee and hip replacements are two of the most commonly performed surgeries in the United States, with more than 1.1 million combined cases performed annually. Depending on patient risk, it is estimated that between 6,000 and 20,000 surgical site infections (SSIs) develop each year in the U.S. after knee and hip replacements, and these numbers, too, are expected to rise."
   >
   > (Hussaini and Martin 2013)

   a  Whose responsibility was it to discuss Mother's level of risk involved in knee replacement surgery? Her primary care physician? The orthopedic surgeon? The family?
   b  After all the time spent with extra procedures ordered by her cardiologist before he would sign the release that Mother was cleared for surgery, should there have been more discussion about Mother's level of risk? Who should have initiated that conversation?

**Recommended research topics**

- Surgical Risk Calculator:

  American College of Surgeons. "Surgical Risk Calculator." Accessed August 9, 2016. http://riskcalculator.facs.org/RiskCalculator/

- Team-Based Care at Mayo Clinic:

  McCarthy, Douglas, Kimberly Mueller, and Jennifer Wrenn. August 2009. "Mayo Clinic: Multidisciplinary Teamwork, Physician-Led Governance, and Patient-Centered Culture Drive World-Class Health Care." *The Commonwealth Fund*, pub 1306, Vol. 27. Accessed August 9, 2016. http://www.commonwealthfund.org/~/media/Files/Publications/Case%20 Study/2009/Aug/1306_McCarthy_Mayo_case%20study.pdf

**Discussion: rehab**

1   I called a 24/7 sitter agency phone line repeatedly without response. What are the communication and coordinated care implications of this?

2   What are the challenges that my sister and I encountered as Mother's caregivers?

3   The rehab home care agency installed telemonitoring equipment.

    a   In what ways was this useful to have in Mother's home?

    b   With the push for Accountable Care Organizations (ACOs), how could the coordination of Mother's care been improved?

        "Accountable Care Organizations (ACOs) are groups of doctors, hospitals, and other health care providers, who come together voluntarily to give coordinated high quality care to their Medicare patients." (CMS, "What's an ACO?")

    c   If the home care nurse had transmitted Mother's vitals for the past week directly to the emergency department, how would that have improved Mother's treatment?

**Recommended research topics**

- Accountable Care Organizations (ACOs):

  Centers for Medicare & Medicaid Services (CMS). "What's an ACO?" Accessed August 7, 2016. https://www.cms.gov/Medicare/Medicare-Fee-for-Service-Payment/ACO/index.html?redirect=/Aco

- Telemonitoring:

  Healthcare Information and Management Systems Society (HIMSS). August 15, 2014. "How Care Is Changing in an #mHealth World." Accessed August 9, 2016. http://www.himss.org/how-care-changing-mhealth-world

## Discussion: emergency

1   Mother spent eight hours in the emergency department. She was transported there from the rehab facility after staff suspected that she was in renal failure.

    a   In what ways could eight hours in the emergency department be justified as patient-centered care?

    b   What was the impact on Mother? On Mother's family? On others in the emergency department, considering she was diagnosed with MRSA?

       "Methicillin-resistant *Staphylococcus aureus* (MRSA) is a bacteria that is resistant to many antibiotics."

(CDC)

2   What benefit was there to keeping Mother in the emergency department versus admitting her right away?

    a   Mother was in the corridor in the emergency department and then admitted to an isolation room. What was the impact – to her and to everyone exposed to her – of keeping her in the corridor?

    b   How could a different suspected diagnosis from the rehab facility have changed Mother's experience, and length of stay, in the emergency department?

## Recommended research topics

•   MRSA (Methicillin-resistant *Staphylococcus aureus*):

    Centers for Disease Control and Prevention (CDC). "Methicillin-resistant *Staphylococcus aureus* (MRSA)." Accessed August 7, 2016. http://www.cdc.gov/mrsa/

•   Precautions to Prevent the Spread of MRSA

    Centers for Disease Control and Prevention (CDC). "Precautions to Prevent the Spread of MRSA." Accessed August 7, 2016. http://www.cdc.gov/mrsa/healthcare/clinicians/precautions.html

## Discussion: hospice

1   An important component of patient-centered care is to give the patient control of their healthcare decisions.

    a   In what ways did Mother exhibit control? Which decisions did she make? Which decisions did she decline to make, or was not given an opportunity to consider?

    b   Which decisions were made for Mother?

2   Discuss why you might have elected (or recommended) surgery instead of hospice?

3   What impact did Mother's visitors have on her (physically, emotionally)?
4   What impact did the setup of Mother's bedroom have on her care and her emotional health?
5   What roles did Mother's two daughters have? What might you have done differently?

## Recommended research topics

- Patient Centered Care:

  Planetree: www.planetree.org

## Discussion: nutrition services

1   In the hospital, how should the meal services have been handled? What would improve the process?
2   How important were the meals for Mother?
3   Discuss the impact on the nursing staff when Mother did not get what she requested?

## Discussion: financial services

Mother's Medicare and AARP secondary coverage were billed for the following services over a five-month period, from June 9 to November 10:

- MRI of the knee to customize the knee prosthesis
- Stress test
- Heart catheterization
- Heart stent
- Circulation tests in both legs
- First surgery: knee replacement
- Second surgery: reopen the knee to clean out the infection (irrigation and debridement)
- First inpatient admission: after knee surgery for five days (as planned)
- Second inpatient admission: after second knee surgery for five days – a readmission within twenty days
- Third inpatient admission: to cardiac isolation room with congestive heart failure for nine days – a readmission within ten days
- First rehab admission: following the first knee surgery (as planned)
- Second rehab admission: following the second knee surgery
- First emergency visit: from home eight days post-discharge from the rehab facility
- Second emergency visit: from the rehab facility during the second stay

In addition, Medicare and AARP were billed for physician fees for these services. Also, Medicare was billed by the Hospice Care Center for home hospice care for six weeks.

**Discussion**

1   Mother experienced both preventable harm and readmission. What impact, financial and otherwise, do you think it had on the hospitals where she was admitted?

> "Medicare spent an estimated $4.4 billion in 2009 to care for patients who had been harmed in the hospital, and readmissions cost Medicare another $26 billion."
>
> (CMS 2011)

2   What is the role of the finance department in educating others about the financial impact to the organization? How are quality and finance integrated in patient care?

3   Who had oversight of Mother's care? Who might have noticed the readmissions from a quality of care perspective? From a hospital revenue penalty perspective? What is that person's responsibility to the patient? To the hospital and/or the insurance company?

**Discussion: conclusion – what happened to my mother?**

1   Discuss how the seven months of care for my Mother were system problems that were not caused by one particular person.

    a   What was the effect of having each person involved in her care function independently? How would that have differed had they used a team approach?

    b   How might the outcome have differed if each person touching her care used a problem-solving approach?

2   How might the outcome have differed if this case followed coordinated care expectations?

3   How might the outcome have differed if this case met Accountable Care expectations?

> "Accountable Care Organizations (ACOs) are groups of doctors, hospitals, and other health care providers, who come together voluntarily to give coordinated high quality care to their Medicare patients."
>
> (CMS, "What's an ACO?")

4   Describe how the cost of Mother's healthcare could have been decreased – could have been considered more affordable.

> "In 2010, Congress enacted the Patient Protection and Affordable Care Act in order to increase the number of Americans covered by health insurance and decrease the cost of health care."
>
> (Supreme Court 2012)

## Bibliography

Centers for Disease Control and Prevention (CDC). "Methicillin-resistant *Staphylococcus aureus* (MRSA)." Accessed August 7, 2016. http://www.cdc.gov/mrsa/Centers for Medicare & Medicaid Services (CMS). "Community-based Care Transitions Program." Accessed August 7, 2016. https://partnershipforpatients.cms.gov/about-the-partnership/community-based-care-transitions-program/community-basedcaretransitionsprogram.html

Centers for Medicare & Medicaid Services (CMS). "What's an ACO?" Accessed August 7, 2016. https://www.cms.gov/Medicare/Medicare-Fee-for-Service-Payment/ACO/index.html?redirect=/Aco

Centers for Medicare & Medicaid Services (CMS). April 29, 2011. "CMS Issues Final Rule for First Year of Hospital Value-Based Purchasing Program." Accessed August 7, 2016. https://www.cms.gov/Newsroom/MediaReleaseDatabase/Fact-sheets/2011-Fact-sheets-items/2011-04-29.html

Hussaini, Anila and Jeff Martin. September/October 2013. "Preventing Infection after Hip and Knee Replacements." *Healthcare Executive*, 28(5):68–70. Accessed August 7, 2016. http://www.ihi.org/resources/Pages/Publications/PreventingInfectionAfterHipKneeReplacements.aspx

Supreme Court of the United States. June 28, 2012. "Decision on the Affordable Care Act." Accessed August 11, 2016. https://www.supremecourt.gov/opinions/11pdf/11-393c3a2.pdf

## Recommended reading and research topics

### Healthcare research

Agency for Healthcare Research and Quality (AHRQ). www.ahrq.gov

### MRSA

Centers for Disease Control and Prevention (CDC). "Methicillin-resistant *Staphylococcus aureus* (MRSA)." Accessed August 7, 2016. http://www.cdc.gov/mrsa/

Centers for Disease Control and Prevention (CDC). "Precautions to Prevent the Spread of MRSA." Accessed August 7, 2016. http://www.cdc.gov/mrsa/healthcare/clinicians/precautions.html

### Patient-centered care

Patient- and Family-Centered Care Organizational Self-Assessment Tool

Institute for Healthcare Improvement and National Institute for Children's Health Quality developed in partnership with the Institute for Patient- and Family-Centered Care. June 2013. "Patient- and Family-Centered Care Organizational Self-Assessment Tool." Accessed August 7, 2016. http://www.ihi.org/resources/Pages/Tools/PatientFamilyCenteredCareOrganizationalSelfAssessmentTool.aspx

Planetree. www.planetree.org

### Patient safety

Joint Commission National Patient Safety Goals. http://www.jointcommission.org/standards_information/npsgs.aspx

### Surgery risk

American College of Surgeons. "Surgical Risk Calculator." Accessed August 9, 2016. http://riskcalculator.facs.org/RiskCalculator/

### Team-based care coordination

McCarthy, Douglas, Kimberly Mueller, and Jennifer Wrenn. August 2009. "Mayo Clinic: Multidisciplinary Teamwork, Physician-Led Governance, and Patient-Centered Culture Drive World-Class Health Care." *The Commonwealth Fund*, pub 1306, Vol. 27. Accessed August 9, 2016. http://www.commonwealthfund.org/~/media/Files/Publications/ Case%20Study/2009/Aug/1306_McCarthy_Mayo_case%20study.pdf

### Telemonitoring

Healthcare Information and Management Systems Society (HIMSS). August 15, 2014. "How Care Is Changing in an #mHealth World." Accessed August 9, 2016. http://www. himss.org/how-care-changing-mhealth-world

### Transforming care at the bedside

Lee, B., D. Shannon, P. Rutherford, and C. Peck. 2008. *Transforming Care at the Bedside How-to Guide: Optimizing Communication and Teamwork*. Cambridge, MA: Institute for Healthcare Improvement. Available at www.IHI.org.

# 3 Human factors: the impact of the workplace

## What is the truth about un-coordinated care?

The "third highest cause of death in the U.S. is medical error" (*Johns Hopkins Medicine* 2016).

By not focusing on the real problem (see Figure 3.1):

- the cost of healthcare will remain high;
- population health efforts will not meet their potential;
- the workforce will be insufficient to meet demand; and
- we will continue to perpetuate tolerance of poor patient outcomes.

The cost of poor quality (COPQ) is calculated by Six Sigma professionals. The metric is defined as "the cost of failing to produce 100 percent quality the first time through" (Harry and Schroeder 2000, 243).

> We don't try to inspect our way to Six Sigma. Rather, we try to eliminate defects at the root source through better processes and better products and service design focused on meeting the needs of the customers. When we aim for this higher standard, we are forced to abandon minor adjustments in how we run our processes and consider entirely new ways of doing business.
>
> (Harry and Schroeder 2000, 35)

Raising process improvement to the strategic level is the pathway to service excellence. At the core of service excellence is quality outcomes. If we improve these basics, then lower cost will follow. Boards and senior executives who lack razor-sharp focus on quality outcomes are missing the mark.

For improved quality outcomes, the physicians and workforce need unrelenting support to accomplish the work they are trained to do. The unique complexity of providing healthcare is due to the high variability of human factors – on both the giving and the receiving end of healthcare services. We have made treatments, procedures, and processes repeatable with reproducible results. However, caregivers are masters of workarounds when they don't have what they need when they need it. Individual workarounds create variability which can lead to errors.

First-time quality requires focus on the work at hand – multitasking is not Lean. If you take the time to observe caregivers, you will notice they are constantly

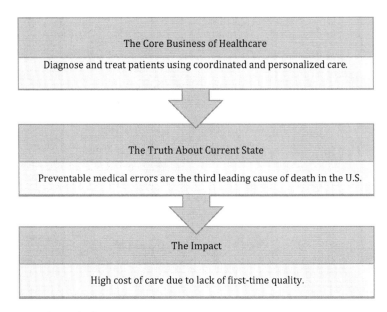

*Figure 3.1* The truth about current state

interrupted; they are pulled in many directions, and they cannot focus on the patient they are with at the moment. Wearable hands-free devices function as excellent communication tools to keep nurses with their patients versus walking around hunting for co-workers. Unfortunately, that has resulted in overutilization of the device creating interruptions to care. As one patient said: "It isn't even important things they are interrupted for." Interruptions break focus and can lead to errors.

## Case study: open heart surgery

While my husband was driving one day, he experienced a brief episode close to blacking out: "dizzy, numb, and trouble seeing," he described. His physician ordered an echocardiogram and a consult with a cardiologist. The results indicated the atrial valve was only functioning at 30 percent and needed to be replaced. My husband questioned why the echocardiogram he had a year prior (due to complaints of extreme fatigue) did not show any issues then. The cardiologist searched for it in the electronic health record and matter of factly said: "oh, my partner read that, and he made a mistake." A cardiac cath was ordered to check for any other problems, and my husband was told that one minor bypass may also be necessary.

A pre-op consult was scheduled with a surgeon. The majority of that visit was spent with a nurse practitioner who later became the one person that my husband and I relied on for help. The delineation of which physician – primary care, cardiologist, heart surgeon – to contact for what issue became confusing.

I was right by my husband's side whenever I was allowed to be there. This gave me the opportunity to observe caregivers at work.

## Observation: interruptions in the intensive care unit (ICU)

Physicians and nurses are assigned a number of patients per day or per shift. How is that number calculated in your organization? Is it based on patient acuity levels? Is it based on quality outcomes research? Is it based on cost? An ICU nurse was heard on the phone saying: "I have no wiggle room" indicating another nurse was needed. That particular nurse was interrupted constantly – she was clearly the "go to" person on the unit. She was training another nurse, called for advice by other staff, while she was caring for my husband after his open heart surgery – and he, the patient, also interrupted her with incessant questioning in his drug-induced state. She was amazing. I learned so much by observing her as I sat in brief spurts in the room with my husband. The most important lesson I learned was that I (as a family member) needed to stay out of her way – out of that room – so she could do her expert work caring for my husband with more tubes and lines coming in and out of him than I have ever seen. She was firm with us as patient and family about what and when things were going to happen based on heart surgery protocols. And, somehow, she remained personable throughout all the interruptions.

## Observation: not speaking up

When my husband was transferred to the telemetry unit, he experienced preventable harm. The nurses throughout the three-night stay provided great care but because they apparently had so many patients assigned to them, my husband's care was handled primarily by assistants. Fortunately, a nurse caught three medication errors sent by pharmacy so there were delays in medication administration. He told me that he was not so fortunate when an assistant came to him rushed to check his blood sugar, and roughly grabbed his arm band for bar coding then got tangled and twisted his IV. She patted down the IV after finishing with the glucometer and left the room. "She didn't even apologize for hurting me," said my husband. Not until the next day when a nurse came to flush out the IV and made my husband's arm burn did he tell what happened and the IV was inserted elsewhere. He was discharged the following day and was told to simply keep an eye on his sore arm.

Four days later, I took him to the cardiology clinic at the hospital – not because of his heart – but because of his arm. It was swollen, hard, red, and warm to touch; was not improving with ice. He said it was burning and hurt worse than his heart surgery incision. I had first called the cardiologist's office at 9:00 a.m. on a Friday and was told that he was booked all day and so were his partners. If my husband had to be seen, I would have to take him to the emergency department. That did not seem appropriate so I called the surgeon's office and spoke with his nurse practitioner. She offered to see him that afternoon, on her day off, even though it was not heart-related. We understood that she was doing us a favor. Who were we supposed to turn to for treatment for harm done in the hospital?

The nurse practitioner said my husband had cellulitis and had to be on antibiotics for ten days. She marked the large area of infection on my husband's arm and said it was important to see his primary care physician on the following Monday to ensure that his arm was improving. I took a photograph of his marked arm and sent it to the nurse manager of the telemetry unit and requested she use that for teaching purposes with the assistant who had not spoken up about disturbing his IV.

At my husband's visit with the surgeon six weeks post-surgery, he was told that his care would transition back to the cardiologist, who had seen him twice in the hospital.

My husband soon started going to cardiac rehab at a different hospital that was closer to home. Since he had been placed on a blood thinner (due to two brief incidences of atrial fibrillation in the hospital) he wore a monitor continuously during the rehab sessions. Results were regularly faxed to his cardiologist.

Three months after surgery, my husband was scheduled for a visit with the cardiologist. Since there had been no further episodes of atrial fibrillation, my husband expected to be taken off the blood thinner. He took copies from all the heart monitoring done at cardiac rehab with him to the visit. The cardiologist denied receiving any reports from rehab; checked the medical records but could not find them; then said they must have been seen by his partner. After reviewing the copies my husband brought, he agreed to discontinue the blood thinner. Since my husband was experiencing some discomfort, he asked the cardiologist for another echocardiogram to ensure everything looked good.

A week after the echocardiogram, my husband placed a call to the cardiologist since he had not heard back about the results. "The valve is functioning appropriately for that type of valve," reported the cardiologist. My husband told the cardiologist that since he kept blaming his partners for oversights and mistakes, he would no longer be his patient and would seek out another cardiologist. Shocked, the cardiologist arrogantly replied: "Do you know who you are talking to? This is Dr. _____."

In addition to blaming his partners, the cardiologist had also blamed my husband's primary care physician for misdiagnosing symptoms. This occurred while my husband was still in the hospital with nurses hearing the comments made, naming the physician. My husband did not appreciate having his primary care physician of sixteen years berated in front of hospital staff. Three incidences of the cardiologist blaming other physicians was clearly not a display of coordinated, team-work behavior.

## Exhausted workforce

The hospital length of stay has decreased significantly over the years, so it is understandable that the pace of care has had to increase. Yet at the same time, there has been a reduction in staff to reduce cost. What we have created is an exhausted workforce. Just watch people nod off in meetings when they finally get to sit down. A previous co-worker of mine described her management work life as "an adrenaline rush." That language was typically used for emergency department employees. But I understood what she meant when I reflected on my management days at the hospital with every day having every minute booked and over two hundred emails to deal with. As soon as I arrived home after a thirty-minute drive, I immediately (after washing my hands, of course) went to my computer to see what emails I had missed. It was hard to enjoy relaxing at home because I was so exhausted. I was not a caregiver and neither was my co-worker, but we experienced that adrenaline rush as a requirement in order to get through each day and then we came down – spent. That is not a healthy routine.

An exhausted workforce – especially caregivers – is dangerous. Concentration is affected and mistakes happen. Perhaps we need to adjust how we calculate and report FTEs: instead of batching all employees together, separate clinical from non-clinical. Much work has been done to not separate employee types in that manner as it is divisive, but when we have such a serious preventable harm rate, we need to consider lowering patient staffing ratios and manager direct reports. Results from a hospital that has done just that, has demonstrated an increase in both employee and patient satisfaction scores while actually improving their bottom line, quality, and safety at the same time.

There is no wonder that we have nursing and primary care physician shortages. With the pressure of so many patients to care for each day, in the clinic or the hospital, it is not an enticing position. I encouraged an acquaintance a few years ago to go for his nursing degree when he expressed his desire to take care of patients instead of working on machinery as an engineer. He was successful in getting the degree and being hired right away at a hospital, but it did not take long for him to get discouraged with the patient load and, as a new nurse, to not have back-up and be left on his own. That did not seem like an environment for him to provide good quality care, so he left, and went back to engineering. How unfortunate that he was passionate about his career change but did not feel the hospital supported him in providing quality care.

## Case study: appendectomy consequences

Patient harm is not always visible or immediate. Often patients don't know enough to speak up or they fear if they do speak up there might be repercussions affecting how they are being treated. So they wait to complain until after they have left the premises.

I had two family members and a friend, residing in three different states, who all had appendectomies within months of each other. My friend was the unlucky one who suffered harm and un-coordinated care. She went to the emergency department and was waiting in her assigned room. She was told she could leave the room to go to the bathroom unassisted, where she passed out, fell, and banged her head and bruised the side of her face. She was taken for a CT-scan of her head while her original abdominal pain continued. They eventually admitted her but not until she said she couldn't take the pain anymore did they finally get her to surgery to remove her appendix. After a few days, the surgeon left for vacation and his associate stopped in briefly each morning.

My dear friend was in the hospital for twelve days for an appendectomy. On the seventh day, her daughter told the nurses that something was not right; her mother was clearly sick and lethargic. Something had to be done. My friend thought she was going to die; and ultimately a nurse determined that my petite friend was not tolerating the morphine. Once that drug was discontinued, she perked up but had problems voiding after having been on a catheter for so long.

Two weeks after discharge, she was readmitted for almost a week with severe pain and then she was told there was nerve damage caused during surgery.

What is the policy for transferring care from one physician to another? Certainly the surgeon deserved his vacation time, but whom did he leave in charge of his patient? Were the hospitalists overextended?

The cost impact of this woman's experience is astounding:

- She passed out and fell, hitting her head and face. Would the hospital be reimbursed for a CT-scan of the head when she presented with abdominal pain, suspected appendicitis?
- A twelve-day hospital stay for an appendectomy is not usual and customary. This most assuredly could have been avoided if she had a coordinated care team who took the time to identify my friend's bad reaction to the morphine. Electronic health record was in place throughout that health system, so why did no one question the excessive length of stay?
- During the two months following her discharge, my friend went to the emergency department two times at a different hospital for severe pain; had repeated CT-scans (since the hospitals didn't share any records). Her primary care physician said the surgeon was the one to handle her post-surgical care, but my friend no longer trusted the surgeon. She didn't know how to resolve the terrible pain, didn't know who was coordinating her care, so she relied on various emergency departments.

In another example of variation in the cost of care, a family member had a laparoscopic appendectomy as an outpatient. She was not admitted for even one night. She went to the emergency department in the morning and was discharged, after surgery, around 9 p.m. I had never heard of an appendectomy as outpatient surgery before, so assumed that cost would be significantly lower. Wrong! The charges totaled $28,000.

My other family member suffered a burst appendix, had laparoscopic surgery also, and was hospitalized for three days. His charges totaled $76,000. That scenario proved to me that $28,000 for outpatient surgery was indeed outrageous.

From the provider's perspective, an appendectomy is not the same for everyone, as just these three very different cases illustrate.

## Observation: medication administration challenges – environmental workarounds

Nurses are to be commended for adapting to their environments to find ways to perform their work swiftly and safely. It is difficult to find work space for medication administration functions at the bedside. With computers for electronic health record access, bar code scanning of patient identification bands and medication packets, nurses need work space that is often insufficient or even nonexistent. The patient's bed may seem the only option for some – thought it's hardly a flat surface with a patient in it and medication packets can easily slide to the floor – but it will do to get the job done. Except when a pill needs to be cut in half. Where can that be done in the room and with what utensil?

When you consider how many times per shift meds are given, this is no trivial matter. These environmental workarounds need attention to facilitate the caregiver's ability to make improvements in patient care. Minor room modifications, equipment and/or technology changes can have a significant impact on the caregiver's ability to administer medications without wasteful (and potentially unsafe) workarounds.

Nurses are historically innovative in making do with what they have. However, that creative effort would be more valuable if spent on finding solutions rather than workarounds. The Institute of Medicine (IOM) defines efficient healthcare in terms of "avoiding waste, including waste of equipment, supplies, ideas and energy" (Institute of Medicine 2001).

**Lean design concepts** include a focus on reducing wasted steps. While shadowing nurses, watch for wasted motion to identify items that need to be relocated closer to the bedside for more efficient and safer medication administration.

Observation of the workplace, piloting process improvements, and mocking up physical environment changes can bring about a quicker understanding of changes needed. After adjustments are made from the trials, then standard work can be developed.

We often fix one thing (the most obvious) without consideration of the other parts of a process. This band-aid approach will not produce the necessary outcome of redesigning the caregiver's work flow. Placement of the meds on the inpatient unit involves multiple disciplines: pharmacy, risk management/safety, nursing, and facilities at a minimum. They must challenge each other to find the safest and most efficient medication administration experience for patients and nurses in their hospital. With the need for four components to come together – medication, electronic health record, bar code scanner, and patient identification band – the physical environment must accommodate the work flow in the sequence it occurs. Don't accept workarounds as just the way the job gets done.

## Assessment of current state: care coordination

The Agency for Healthcare Research and Quality (AHRQ) gives the following examples of specific care coordination activities:

- "Establishing accountability and agreeing on responsibility
- Communicating/sharing knowledge
- Helping with transitions of care
- Assessing patient needs and goals
- Creating a proactive care plan
- Monitoring and follow-up, including responding to changes in patients' needs
- Supporting patients' self-management goals

- Linking to community resources
- Working to align resources with patient and population needs"
  (AHRQ: http://www.ahrq.gov/professionals/prevention-chronic-care/
  improve/coordination/index.html. Accessed August 9, 2016)

Using the specific care coordination activities listed here, I developed a survey tool for nurses and recommendations based on the scores (see Tables 3.1 and 3.2). That tool, in combination with interview questions (see Table 3.3), exposes the current-state experience of your nurses. The value of these tools depends on honest responses, so how they are administered and by whom is important.

*Table 3.1* Assessment of current state: care coordination

Check all that apply: □ RN   □ BSN   □ MSN   □ Other (Please Specify): _____
Work Environment: □ Clinic   □ Hospital - Inpatient   □ Hospital - Outpatient

**ASSESSMENT OF CURRENT STATE CARE COORDINATION**

Please circle the number that is the closest match to your current situation.

| Examples of specific care coordination activities[1] | I am not comfortable | Needs to improve | Improvements underway | Works well most of the time | Best practice | N/A or Don't Know |
|---|---|---|---|---|---|---|
| | 1 | 2 | 3 | 4 | 5 | X |
| 1 Establishing accountability and agreeing on responsibility | 1 | 2 | 3 | 4 | 5 | X |
| 2 Communicating/sharing knowledge | 1 | 2 | 3 | 4 | 5 | X |
| 3 Helping with transitions of care | 1 | 2 | 3 | 4 | 5 | X |
| 4 Assessing patient needs and goals | 1 | 2 | 3 | 4 | 5 | X |
| 5 Creating a proactive care plan | 1 | 2 | 3 | 4 | 5 | X |
| 6 Monitoring and followup, including responding to changes in patients' needs | 1 | 2 | 3 | 4 | 5 | X |
| 7 Supporting patients' self-management goals | 1 | 2 | 3 | 4 | 5 | X |
| 8 Linking to community resources | 1 | 2 | 3 | 4 | 5 | X |
| 9 Working to align resources with patient and population needs       Total | 1 | 2 | 3 | 4 | 5 | X |

[1]Retrieved at:
http://www.ahrq.gov/professionals/prevention-chronic-care/improve/coordination/index.html

*Table 3.2* Assessment recommendations

| SCORE | RECOMMENDATIONS |
|---|---|
| 18 or less | Time to intervene. Observation is important for clarity of the issues. Prioritize improvement initiatives. |
| 19–27 | Clear goals and expectations are needed with an action plan. Be sure to include a time line. |
| 28–36 | Appear to be heading in the right direction. Ensure status updates are scheduled and improvements continue. |
| 37–45 | Good job! Share learnings throughout the organization and externally where relevant. |
| N/A or Don't Know | Question why an item was marked 'N/A' or 'Don't Know.' Should those be explored further? Is training needed? |

*Table 3.3* Coordinated care interview questions

| COORDINATED CARE INTERVIEW | |
|---|---|
| DATE: _____ | |
| TITLE OF PERSON INTERVIEWED: _____ | |
| TYPE OF ORGANIZATION: _____ | |
| 1  How would you define coordinated care? | Response: |
| 2  Give an example of good coordinated care from your own experience. | Response: |
| 3  Describe experiences when you felt there were barriers to coordinated care? What types of barriers? | Response: |
| 4  Describe your department's (organization's) attitude toward coordinated care. | Response: |
| 5  If you could improve coordinated care in your particular department, what would you change? | Response: |

## Impact on human factors

Great strides have been made in transitioning from blaming individuals to analyzing systems in place that contribute to errors. The workplace environment, staffing models, and safety culture are three important areas of focus that have an impact on human factors.

- Workplace Environment

The Joint Commission's "Human Factors Analysis in Patient Safety Systems" states:

> "We have to look at the environment or the physical conditions that contributed to an error," says Wyatt (earlier identified as Ronald Wyatt, MD, medical director, Office of Quality and Patient Safety at The Joint Commission). "The noise level, the lighting, distractions, how equipment is designed, the characteristics and steps involved in the task, and even how the culture contributes to the error."
> (The Joint Commission 2015)

- Staffing Models

With all the great intentions of individual healthcare professionals to deal with daily workloads, management's staffing policies and procedures are tied to patient outcomes. API Healthcare Corporation's "Lessening the Negative Impact of Human Factors" states:

> Long-term workforce management strategies and short-term staffing decisions have a profound impact on patient outcomes.
> (API Healthcare Corporation 2015)

- Safety Culture

The Joint Commission's "Patient Safety Systems" chapter states:

> In a strong safety culture, the hospital has an unrelenting commitment to safety and to do no harm. Among the most critical responsibilities of hospital leaders is to establish and maintain a strong safety culture within their hospital.
> (The Joint Commission 2016)

## Bibliography

Agency for Healthcare Research and Quality (AHRQ). "Care Coordination." Accessed August 9, 2016. http://www.ahrq.gov/professionals/prevention-chronic- care/improve/coordination/index.html

API Healthcare Corporation. 2015. "Lessening the Negative Impact of Human Factors: Linking Staffing Variables and Patient Outcomes." Accessed August 13, 2016. https://www.apihealthcare.com/sites/default/files/Lessening%20the%20Negative %20Impact%20of%20Human%20Factors%20-%20JB33305US.pdf

Harry, Michael and Richard Schroeder. 2000. *Six Sigma: The Breakthrough Management Strategy Revolutionizing the World's Top Corporations*. New York: Doubleday.

Institute of Medicine. 2001. "Crossing the Quality Chasm: A New Health System for the 21st Century." Report Brief by National Academy of Sciences. Accessed August 9, 2016. https://www.nationalacademies.org/hmd/~/media/Files/Report%20Files/2001/ Crossing-the-Quality- Chasm/Quality%20Chasm%202001%20%20report%20brief.pdf

Johns Hopkins Medicine. 2016. "Study Suggests Medical Errors Now Third Leading Cause of Death in the U.S." http://www.hopkinsmedicine.org/news/media/releases/study_suggests_medical_errors_now_third_leading_cause_of_death_in_the_us

The Joint Commission. April 2015. "Human Factors Analysis in Patient Safety Systems." *The Source*, 13(4). Accessed August 13, 2016. www.jointcommission.org

The Joint Commission. January 2016. "Patient Safety Systems (PS)." *Comprehensive Accreditation Manual for Hospitals (CAMH)*, Update 2. Accessed August 13, 2016. www.jointcommission.org

Makary, Martin A. and Michael Daniel. 2016. "Medical Error – The Third Leading Cause of Death in the US." *BMJ*, 353(i2139). doi:10.1136/bmj.i2139

# Part II

# A strategic approach toward eliminating preventable harm

Part I highlighted the impact of un-coordinated care on the patient, family, and caregivers.

Part II transitions to instruction on how to raise process improvement to a strategic level in order to eliminate preventable harm.

Chapter 4 focuses on the role of executives that must be structured to not only support but lead this change effort.

Chapters 5 and 6 detail the implementation of *Process Improvement Strategy Deployment* (Morrill © 2012).

# 4 Leading change

The many facets of the healthcare executive's role must be grounded in serving as a coach: having a thorough understanding of what the team has to accomplish; knowing how the team is actually performing; ensuring that team members get the training and resources they need to perform at the highest level; then letting the team do what you hired them to do. As coach, setting the expectation of continually seeking improvement is of utmost importance. This requires executive commitment and structure to stay involved with improvement progression.

Notable examples of healthcare leader behavior include the following:

- A chief operating officer who fully trusted her employees to do their work and to seek her help if/when needed. This worked well because she was clear in her expectations; and she asked physicians, employees, and her own executive peers for their help when needed. She modeled the behavior she expected of others.
- A hospital president who knew she needed to embark on a building project to upgrade the inpatient units, but first worked on addressing morale issues and staff turnover on the units. An executive who clearly understood the priorities.
- A chief financial officer who kicked off an improvement initiative telling employees that she had no idea where the effort was going to lead, but she was excited to get started. Her transparency in not knowing the solutions and her eagerness to improve set the tone to both engage and motivate employees.
- A hospital president brought in as head of a new venture that had already been planned and was being implemented. He fully investigated the planning models and brought on advisers to test assumptions and to help him develop a new management framework and innovative operational models while he recruited his leadership team. His ability to seek input while challenging traditional thinking was an inspiration for generating new ideas.

## Start with respect

The foundation of Lean is respect for people. These healthcare executives are leaders who clearly demonstrate respect for people at all levels of their organizations. They know how to lead change and build relationships.

Do your employees share their ideas for improvement? Do they feel respected? If we ignore input over and over again or in any way belittle, that slams the door on open communication. In general, healthcare is a demanding, hectic, and exhausting environment to work in; adding disrespectful and intimidating relationships to the mix makes an unhealthy culture.

"Maslow's (1943, 1954) hierarchy of needs includes five motivational needs, often depicted as hierarchical levels within a pyramid. This five stage model can be divided into basic and psychological needs which ensure survival (e.g. physiological, safety, love, and esteem) and growth needs (self-actualization)" (McLeod 2016). Employees who can't get past the first three levels are not going to have the self-esteem to speak up and share with others. They will not be able to realize their full potential (Maslow's highest level of self-actualization).

The Joint Commission includes 'respect' in their "Comprehensive Accreditation Manual for Hospitals:"

> In an integrated patient safety system, staff and leaders work together to eliminate complacency, promote collective mindfulness, treat each other with respect and compassion, and learn from their patient safety events, including close calls and other system failures that have not yet led to patient harm.
>
> (The Joint Commission 2016)

For a description of how to build a culture of respect, read:

- Balle, M. and F. Balle. 2014. *Lead with Respect: A Novel of Lean Practice.* Cambridge: Lean Enterprise Institute.

## Change readiness

Organizations and their executives are at varying stages of readiness for change. An apparent gap in leading change is making the change itself discussable. Openly addressing the difficulty of the change and the impact on those involved makes a significant difference in building relationships for successful implementation.

First, executives need to assess the impact of the change on themselves:

- *What is the impact on me? Personally? Professionally?*
- *How willing am I to change?*
- *Are the feelings I have about this change clouding my judgment and affecting my leadership?*

Leading the depth of change necessary to improve the poor quality associated with preventable medical harm being the third leading cause of death raises the need for enhanced leadership talent. Consider this self-assessment:

- *How do I foster relationships?*
- *How respectful am I?*

- *In what ways am I actively raising the level of urgency of change?*
- *How often do I take action?*
- *In what ways do I assess the impact of change?*
- *Do I see and listen to what is the reality of the current state?*
- *Do I truly understand the impact on individuals and on the organization?*
- *Have I developed new skills myself for driving performance?*
- *In what ways do I encourage development of others?*
- *Do I budget funds and time to support a continuous learning culture?*

Assess and rate your current skills (see Figure 4.1) so you can build your change leadership plan.

To assess change readiness of teams, I have used the SWOT (Strengths/Weaknesses/Opportunities/Threats) analysis to assess readiness at various stages by simply asking teams to answer: "How ready are you for _____?" (fill in the blank with whatever improvement or project you are planning to implement). Using a 10-point scale over time to rate each quadrant helps you see the improvement in readiness for a significant change at the various stages of assessment.

Delving deeper to find a better way to assess readiness by researching methodologies and then interviewing a few change management professionals, the following sources stand out:

- DICE ASSESSMENT: Duration/Integrity/Commitment/Effort

  Sirkin, H. L., P. Keenan, and A. Jackson. Winter 2014. "The Hard Side of Change Management." *Harvard Business Review OnPoint* (originally published in October 2005).

- Oliver Wight International, Inc. 2010. *The Oliver Wight Class A Checklist for Business Excellence*, Sixth Edition. John Wiley & Sons.
- CHANGE STYLE INDICATOR: Improve Change Effectiveness

  Discovery Learning, Inc. at www.discoverylearning.com

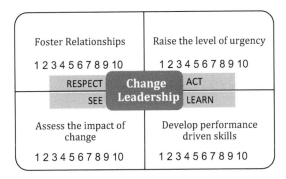

*Figure 4.1* Change leadership self-assessment, Morrill (2016)

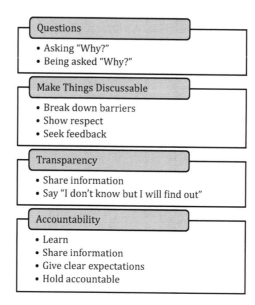

*Table 4.1* Problem-solving culture

## Problem-solving culture

Change leaders need to promote a problem-solving culture (see Table 4.1) which builds the platform for continuous improvement.

What does a problem-solving culture look like? Every level of the organization is asking others why things are done a certain way. Staff members feel they have permission – feel empowered – to make things discussable. Silos are fading with more transparency across departments. We are all learning together how to do things differently so we must ask questions with respect and open discussion. In order to make lasting improvements happen we must put problem-solving tools in the hands of all staff and then we can hold each other accountable.

## Accountability

Who is watching the results of improvement initiatives in your organization? Are the expected outcomes realized and within the time frame identified? Consider creating a results committee, as one exemplary change leader hospital president developed. Lean and Six Sigma improvement efforts were clearly linked to their strategic plan and the multidisciplinary committee came together to assess metrics and outcomes.

A project manager with business analysis experience on staff should be able to develop a structured methodology to align with your problem-solving culture to assess performance of initiatives underway and launched. A project manager in coordination with results committee members should serve as coaches (and cheerleaders) to the leadership accountable for the initiatives to help with course correction, realignment of priorities, etc.

Do not make the mistake of relying on any one committee to eliminate patient harm. A results committee can provide valuable oversight of improvement progress but the responsibility of problem solving at the point of patient care lies in the hands of each caregiver and their support teams. That is why it is vital that executives get involved and provide the training and the coaching needed to empower the workforce with daily problem-solving talent.

Shared accountability can be a relief; to have team members to problem solve with and to make more informed decisions together. However, that does require trust. "Trust is not only the fruit of trustworthiness; it is also the root of motivation. It is the highest form of motivation" (Covey 2004, 181). Change leaders are often told they have to engage and motivate their people, but more effort is needed on building relationships and building trust.

Consider how organizational governance and finance structures actually create barriers to coordinated, interdisciplinary, team-based care. Patient volumes, operational expenses, and leadership are all delineated by department thereby creating rewards and reprimands from narrow viewpoints. Budgets actually drive care decisions more than we want to admit. For example, moving nurses from one cost center to another for a shift raises resistance from managers who don't want labor cost overages even if the move would create a better nurse to patient staffing ratio. Management accountability needs to shift to decision making for the good of the patient and the organization versus the department. The structures in place influence attitude, behavior, and overall culture that either promote or discourage interdisciplinary interaction.

A continuous learning environment combined with accountability is the combination required for relentless efforts toward eliminating harm.

## Step up and take action

> An excellent definition of leadership is that it creates the environment in which others can self-actualize in the process of completing the task. In short, good leaders develop other leaders.
>
> (Townsend and Gebhardt 2008, 11)

The following two chapters give you a guide for how to raise process improvement to a strategic level in your organization. Without a strategic focus on eliminating preventable harm, efforts will fall short, excuses and tolerance will continue. Step up and take action to lead the depth of transformation required to bring about positive change in medical errors and harm statistics.

## Bibliography

Covey, Stephen R. 2004. *The 8th Habit: From Effectiveness to Greatness*. New York: Free Press.

McLeod, S. A. 2016. "Maslow's Hierarchy of Needs." *Simply Psychology*. Accessed August 9, 2016. http://www.simplypsychology.org/maslow.html

Morrill, Patricia. 2016. "Injecting the Fundamentals of Change into Healthcare." Presented at the *ASQ Lean and Six Sigma Conference*, Phoenix, March 1.

The Joint Commission. January 2016. "Patient Safety Systems (PS)." In *Comprehensive Accreditation Manual for Hospitals (CAMH)*, Update 2. Accessed August 13, 2016. www.jointcommission.org

Townsend, Patrick L. and Joan E. Gebhardt. 2008. *How Organizations Learn: Investigate, Identify, Institutionalize*. Milwaukee, WI: ASQ Quality Press.

## Recommended reading and research topics

### Change readiness

Discovery Learning, Inc. "Change Style Indicator: Improve Change Effectiveness." Accessed August 9, 2016. www.discoverylearning.com

Oliver Wight International, Inc. 2010. *The Oliver Wight Class A Checklist for Business Excellence*, Sixth Edition. Hoboken, NJ: Wiley.

Sirkin, H. L., P. Keenan, and A. Jackson. Winter 2014. "The Hard Side of Change Management." *Harvard Business Review OnPoint* (originally published in October 2005).

### Leadership

Covey, Stephen R. 2004. *The 8th Habit: From Effectiveness to Greatness*. New York: Free Press.

Dudley, Drew. 2010. "Leading with Lollipops." *TEDxToronto*. Accessed August 16, 2016. www.youtube.com

### Respect

Balle, M. and F. Balle. 2014. *Lead with Respect: A Novel of Lean Practice*. Cambridge: Lean Enterprise Institute.

# 5   A guide to *Process Improvement Strategy Deployment*

## What can *you* do?

## Introduction

In Chapter 1, an intimate view is shared illustrating the impact of preventable harm.

Chapter 2 provides probing questions for you and your team about the events and interactions that occurred in Chapter 1 and how the actions did or did not support coordinated care.

Chapter 3 focuses on healthcare providers and the challenges they face in high-pressured environments.

Chapter 4 highlights the role of executives in leading change.

Chapter 5 transitions to a guidebook approach. The intent of this chapter is to assist healthcare organizations in picking up the pace for improvements in patient outcomes, satisfaction, and cost reduction. *Process Improvement Strategy Deployment* (Morrill 2012) is a 10-step model integrating Lean and project management methodologies for developing a problem-solving culture and for raising process improvement to a strategic level. This approach helps your leadership team focus on the right priorities and assist all levels of the organization in understanding:

- the value of their work,
- how their work relates to the strategic plan, and
- their accountability for improvement.

There are many excellent instructional resources on the market detailing Lean and project management methodologies. Lean is defined as "a systematic approach to identifying and eliminating waste (non-value-added activities) through continuous improvement by flowing the product at the pull of the customer in pursuit of perfection" (Manos and Vincent, editors 2012, 390). Many healthcare organizations have seen significant improvements in business, financial, clinical, and operational processes by implementing Lean methods.

This guidebook serves as an introduction to the *integration* of these methodologies to enhance performance – to make change happen more quickly. Throughout this section, recommended reading references are provided.

## Application in practice: integrating Lean and project management at Monroe Clinic

In 2008, I had the pleasure of assisting Monroe Clinic in kicking off their Lean journey. Monroe Clinic, in Monroe, Wisconsin, is an integrated, not-for-profit, single hospital health system with multi-specialty physician practices and eleven locations serving communities in Wisconsin and Illinois.

I returned in 2011 for a seven-month engagement to provide leadership development in advanced problem solving by integrating Lean and project management methodologies. As an organizational initiative tied to their strategic plan, championed by the vice president of Service Excellence & Process Improvement in partnership with human resources, all ninety-two leaders (coaches, directors, administration, including the CEO) were required to participate in this leadership-development effort.

As leaders practicing a new coaching model at the time and learning about leader standard work, they brought forth real problems with the expectation of leading the implementation of change to improve processes. Through the experience of working closely and coaching these leaders in both group and individual settings, a common thread of challenges emerged – action steps for implementing change. Often, their issues were not broken down into manageable components, causing participants angst in where and how to begin. Light bulb moments started happening when they learned how to 'bucket' tasks that could be sequenced, phased, and delegated. By using project management methodologies to support their Lean process improvement initiatives, they were able to begin taking manageable steps to improve processes.

Leaders represented all areas of the hospital and clinics and their problems varied widely with multiple levels of complexities. Some of the improvements they worked on that were tied to the organization's strategic plan were:

- Improve patient experience by having lab and imaging available in branch settings.
- Gain efficiency by combining clinic and hospital phlebotomy services.
- Decrease costs related to disappearing linens.
- Improve time utilization by reducing the number of times non-English speaking patients miss appointments.
- Improve the quality of the surgery pre-op process for total joints.

Today, Monroe Clinic is more committed than ever to their Lean journey and accelerated efforts to develop their leaders.

> As leaders, we began to recognize that process improvement isn't just about the tools, it's about leadership. We needed a different way to lead, and with a sense of urgency, embarked on the next phase of learning on our Lean journey.
> (Vice President of Service Excellence & Process Improvement, Monroe Clinic, 2015)

Monroe Clinic's ongoing commitment to leading process improvement through staff development in problem solving is a shining example of a learning culture that enables and engages the people who do the work.

My Mother's story (Chapter 1) was first used as an example of un-coordinated care with Monroe Clinic leaders. Their overwhelming appreciation for sharing her case study encouraged me to continue using it in my work with other clients. Reflecting on the leadership development experience with Monroe Clinic, I realized the need for a guide that combines Lean and project management in order to drive change in healthcare. I developed the 10-step *Process Improvement Strategy Deployment* model.

## The *Process Improvement Strategy Deployment* model

Does your organization work on strategic planning and process improvement initiatives on separate tracks where executives in the boardroom produce vision and great ideas, then staff are told to go forth and solve world hunger? The *Process Improvement Strategy Deployment* model presented in this chapter encourages an entirely different approach. Process improvement initiatives consume resources that must be managed: selection, prioritization, and scheduling in concert with the overall organizational strategic efforts.

Strategy or policy deployment, *hoshin kanri*, is defined as "a management process that aligns – both vertically and horizontally – a firm's functions and activities with its strategic objectives. The objective is to match available resources with desirable projects so that only projects that are desirable, important, and achievable are authorized" (Lean Enterprise Institute 2004, 61).

*Hoshin kanri* is "a strategic planning system developed in Japan and North America over the past thirty years. Also known as strategic policy deployment. Metaphorical meanings include 'ship in a storm going in the right direction' and 'shining needle or compass'" (Dennis 2007, 160).

The whitepaper *Strategy Deployment* gives this description: "Unlike traditional planning, it's not an annual exercise but an iterative approach for transformation and continuous improvement." The paper does an excellent job stating the need for strategy deployment:

> Even in a small organization, there are always too many things to accomplish, too few resources, and too many distractions. Strategy deployment focuses and aligns an organization on those goals most meaningful systemwide, connecting them to the actual work that delivers value to patients, and spurring meaningful and systematic conversations about how those goals should be tackled.
>
> (ThedaCare Center for Healthcare Value 2011)

## The executive's role in leading change

I first learned about *hoshin* in 1995 working with a large healthcare system embarking on a merger with another multi-campus system. Our CEO introduced the methodology to our management team, providing clarity about the organizational goals for the year. We were to concentrate on the business functions – HR, finance, purchasing – across campuses and to stay away from patient care. We knew where to focus our efforts as we faced a multitude of changes with the merger.

## The ten steps of *Process Improvement Strategy Deployment*

The *Process Improvement Strategy Deployment* 10-step model (see Figure 5.1) is iterative and scalable for any size organization; depending on the size and complexity of your healthcare entity you may focus more on certain sectors.

### *Step 1: ensure high-level understanding of current state*

Step 1 sounds easy and many organizations just jump right into Step 2 – Develop Strategic Plan making assumptions that they fully understand what is going on in their business and clinical units. In fact, your toughest assignment at any level of the organization is to define what is actually happening – not how it is supposed to be. How are customers truly being served? How much time and money is being wasted?

The day-to-day bombardment of all the things to do right away (and do more with less) permeates throughout all levels so that a flurry of activity is what we see. And, if you don't look busy then perhaps you aren't adding value. One CEO expected everyone to be so busy they were *breathless*. Really? No wonder it is difficult to make changes if we are expected to be exhausted in carrying out our daily work. How can we possibly become problem solvers in that environment? How can we move to relationship-based care, personalized care, coordinated care in that pressure cooker workplace?

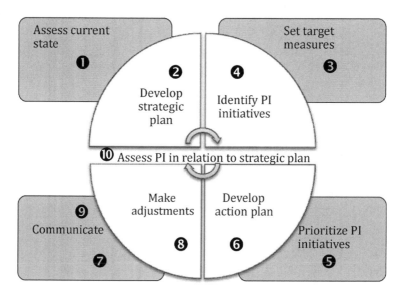

*Figure 5.1 Process Improvement Strategy Deployment* model

Knowing your current state means more than studying dashboards. There is no data that gives a true picture of patient/staff/physician interactions and experiences. It is not enough to know *what* is happening; you have to know *how* the work is carried out – that is the culture piece, your key to engaging continuous improvement . . . continuous problem solving.

## Step 1: action steps

- Value stream mapping

    ◦ Each department should have a value stream map (see Figure 5.2) posted in their area illustrating how they serve their customers – identifying key process steps.

    ◦ Begin with the key process steps to prepare the value stream map (see Figure 5.3).

    ◦ Next, information flow shows what key communication methods are linked to which process steps, if any (see Figure 5.4).

    ◦ The amount of time it takes for each process step is entered (see Figure 5.5). It is helpful in some departments to include a time line: this example shows a two-hour time line for an appointment.

    ◦ Getting to the real story. Adding the wait times makes it clear where delays occur and reveals why the expected time line (two hours in this example) is not being met (see Figure 5.6).

Using visual indicator boards in every department with value stream maps and clear action steps needed helps everyone stay focused on where they need to get to for improved customer service.

- Observation

    ◦ Leadership should be able to access this information readily; and preferably on a Gemba Walk (going directly to the place where value is created), asking questions and talking with staff. All staff should know the key points of their gap analysis: where they are currently, where they need to get to, and what they are doing about it.

    ◦ When was the last time you stepped away from your desk and took a walk to the areas you are responsible for to watch how staff work while asking questions to fully understand where and why they are struggling in performance of customer expectations?

    ◦ Is it clear to everyone what the expectations are? It is human nature to want to be successful in achieving certain goals. If expectations are not clearly defined, if the target is unknown, then most certainly the road to improvement will be slow.

    ◦ Nothing takes the place of observation. Going to see what is actually occurring and asking questions is the only true way to replace erroneous assumptions.

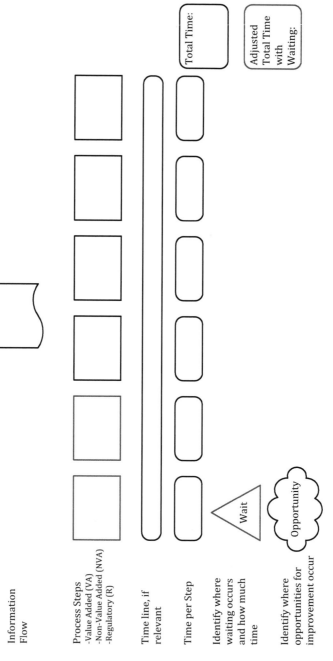

Information
Flow

Process Steps
-Value Added (VA)
-Non-Value Added (NVA)
-Regulatory (R)

Time line, if
relevant

Time per Step

Identify where
waiting occurs
and how much
time

Identify where
opportunities for
improvement occur

Wait

Opportunity

Total Time:

Adjusted
Total Time
with
Waiting:

*Figure 5.2* Step 1: value stream mapping – overview

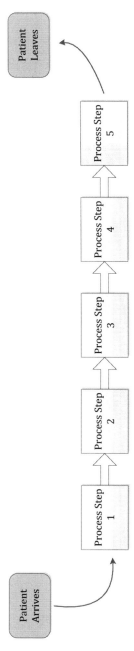

*Figure 5.3* Step 1: value stream mapping – process steps

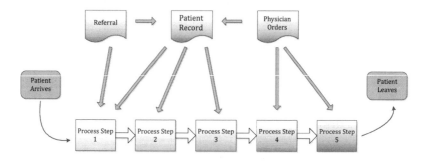

*Figure 5.4* Step 1: value stream mapping – information flow

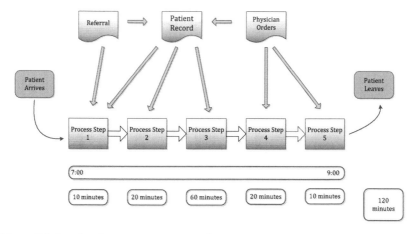

*Figure 5.5* Step 1: value stream mapping – time per step

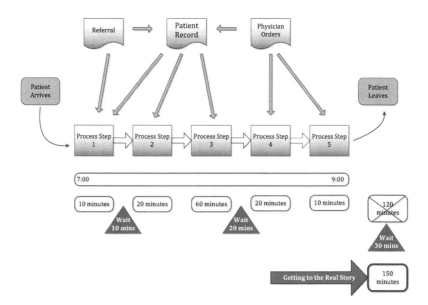

*Figure 5.6* Step 1: value stream mapping – getting to the real story

- Educating senior leaders on the reality of the current state – the starting point – is an important precursor to strategic planning efforts. Grounding executives in true performance sets the stage for more robust strategic goals for the short-term (e.g., first year of a five-year plan) to prepare the organization for a framework that successfully advances performance. This approach is based in a change management culture and alerts the organization to accountability requirements.

### Recommended reading for step 1

Rother, Mike and John Shook. 2009. *Learning to See: Value-Stream Mapping to Create Value and Eliminate Muda*. Version 1.4. Cambridge: Lean Enterprise Institute.
Zidel, Thomas G. 2006. *A Lean Guide to Transforming Healthcare*. Milwaukee: ASQ Quality Press.

### Step 2: develop strategic plan

How do you know what is critical for your business to focus on in the strategic plan without knowing the truth about how you are performing?

As part of your strategic planning process, be sure to address the topic of preventable medical harm in your organization. What situations are occurring that have the potential for harm? Which patient outcomes data need attention? Set the tone at the strategic level that eliminating patient harm is the first priority.

Consider formal risk assessments after poor-performing situations become more obvious during current-state (Step 1) exploration. Whether faced with clinical, business, financial, or physical environment risks, the Failure Modes & Effects Analysis (FMEA) risk assessment process is valuable. One department's problem should be raised to an organizationwide problem to solve where risk is involved.

Do you have incentives in place that are tied to organizational performance? Results can be rapid when all on the management team are partially compensated for key performance indicators. Frequent closures of emergency departments in a health system quickly stopped once a CEO made clear that it was not just the emergency department's problem to turn around, it was an organizationwide issue and he tied it to management compensation. Another CEO actually had all employees benefit from quarterly payouts if key performance indicators were met.

What really matters is a clear focus from the top leaders. Limiting the number of strategic plan goals (see Figure 5.7) takes leadership discipline. It is necessary

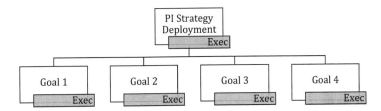

*Figure 5.7* Step 2: strategic plan goals

to do so in order to keep the organization focused on what is important . . . and to be clear about the expectation of accountability and accomplishment.

Now, of course, everyone wants to jump to that action plan with tactics for each strategic goal, right? Making assumptions about where we are and where we need to get to is typical. But first the gap analysis is necessary to help everyone get on the same page about reality – the truth. That requires transparency and exposure.

## Step 2: action steps

•   Limit your strategic plan goals to four or five

*Recommended reading for step 2*

Kenagy, John. 2009. *Designed to Adapt: Leading Healthcare in Challenging Times.* Bozeman, MT: Second River Healthcare Press.

McChesney, Chris, Sean Covey, and Jim Huling. 2012. *The 4 Disciplines of Execution: Achieving Your Wildly Important Goals.* New York: Simon & Schuster.

Ries, Eric. 2011. *The Lean Startup: How Today's Entrepreneurs Use Continuous Improvement to Create Radically Successful Businesses.* New York: Crown Business.

Toussaint, John and Roger A. Gerard. 2010. *On the Mend: Revolutionizing Healthcare to Save Lives and Transform the Industry.* Cambridge: Lean Enterprise Institute.

## *Step 3: set target measures*

Once you honestly understand how you are performing and know strategically where you need to be heading to reach your goal, then you can start identifying the target measures. The gap analysis provides a mechanism for the early communication and identification of process improvement initiatives. That transparency, however, doesn't merely provide measurements for the sake of measuring. That would just create information overload. Be clear about the focus. What's important? Select a few key performance indicators.

Extensive effort is often spent on creating charts and graphs, but who analyzes them? Even though the data starts looking better when the measures head in the right direction, who is checking to make sure the outcomes have really improved? You might be measuring the wrong thing, trying to fix the wrong problem.

Do you have *data fatigue*? Do you wonder how anything can be fixed? It can be overwhelming. My Lean and Six Sigma colleagues are probably getting pretty nervous reading this, so I will clarify. Data is helpful and useful; it is absolutely essential when making your case for something that needs to change. A visual illustration eliminates the emotion that it is one person's opinion, rather it makes a data-driven case.

My point is that you need to be sure that you are measuring what matters, what correlates with the problem at hand. This often means collecting data you haven't studied before; asking finance, quality, decision support staff to track certain metrics needed for your improvement initiative analysis.

**Step 3: action steps**

- Gather baseline measures
- Investigate relevant benchmarks
- Perform gap analysis

*Recommended reading for step 3*

Cunningham, Jean and Orest Fiume. 2003. *Real Numbers: Management Accounting in a Lean Organization.* Durham, NC: Managing Times Press.

Manos, Anthony and Chad Vincent, editors. 2012. *The Lean Handbook: A Guide to the Bronze Certification Body of Knowledge.* Milwaukee, WI: ASQ Quality Press.

### *Step 4: identify key process improvement initiatives*

Based on the gap analysis, process improvement (PI) initiatives will become clear. Figure 5.8 is one way to depict which PI initiatives are linked to the strategic plan. A clear visual gives the entire organization a full understanding of what is important to achieve and how to help each other.

Still at a high level, the development of charters and Lean A3 problem-solving tools can be started.

The charter (see Figure 5.9) defines the issue: why it is important, what is and what is not within scope, the expected outcomes, team members, and a preliminary plan.

Lean A3 problem solving is defined as: "A Toyota-pioneered practice of getting the problem, the analysis, the corrective actions, and the action plan down on a single sheet of large (A3) paper, often with the use of graphics" (Lean Enterprise Institute 2004). The A3 problem-solving tool (see Figure 5.10) can begin at this stage with high-level information about background, current state, and some preliminary targets. The root cause is to be investigated later during more detailed analysis. This one-pager is another excellent communication device used to tell the story to all involved.

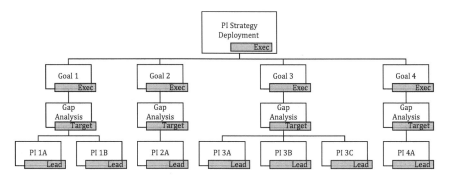

*Figure 5.8* Steps 3 and 4: gap analysis and process improvement (PI) initiatives

**Project Charter**: *(Name)*

| Business Case: *(Why is this important to work on? How does this link to the strategic plan?)* | |
| --- | --- |
| Problem/Opportunity: | Scope, Constraints, Assumptions: *(What is not within the scope?)* |
| Goal: *(Expected outcomes)* | Stakeholders: |
| | Team: |

| Preliminary Project Plan | Target Dates / Budget | Actual Dates / Budget |
| --- | --- | --- |
| | | |

| Prepared by: | Approved by: |
| --- | --- |

*Figure 5.9* Step 4: project charter

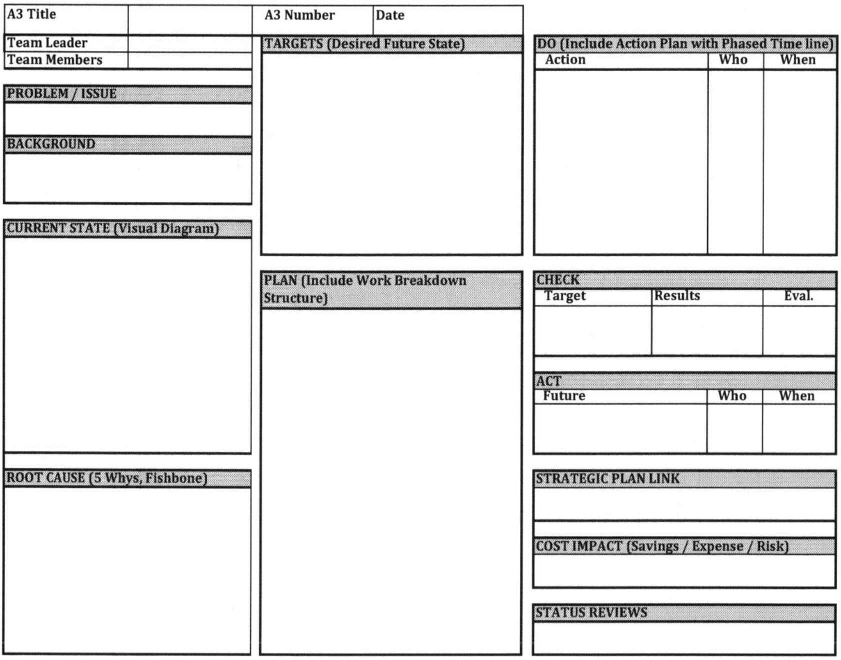

*Figure 5.10* Step 4: A3 problem-solving tool

## Step 4: action steps

- Charter
- A3 initiation
- Value stream mapping
- SWOT analysis

*Recommended reading for step 4*

Graban, Mark. 2009. *Lean Hospitals: Improving Quality, Patient Safety, and Employee Satisfaction.* New York: Productivity Press.

Manos, Anthony and Chad Vincent, editors. 2012. *The Lean Handbook: A Guide to the Bronze Certification Body of Knowledge.* Milwaukee, WI: ASQ Quality Press.

## *Step 5: prioritize process improvement initiatives*

Organizations must be more intentional in order to achieve success with strategic planning. Several tools are listed here: project management (work breakdown structure, sequencing, scheduling, resource allocation), risk assessment (FMEA), and criteria prioritization (selection matrix, other organizational initiatives). Failing to complete step 5, we cannot provide clarity about what is important and where the entire organization should focus. We take our eyes off productivity.

How are improvement initiatives selected in your organization?

Work breakdown structure (WBS) is defined as "a method of subdividing work into smaller and smaller increments to permit accurate estimates of durations, resource requirements, and costs" (Lewis 2001, 530).

"A company should take the agreed-upon strategic plan and break it down like a work breakdown structure (WBS). Not only will this force the understanding of what each strategic initiative means, it will also solidify the path to achieve it" (Morris 2010, 22).

## Step 5: action steps

- Work breakdown structure (WBS), see Figure 5.11
- Sequencing

  ○ What needs to happen first?

- Scheduling

  ○ In which month(s) or quarter(s) should an initiative begin?

- FMEA (Failure Modes & Effects Analysis) risk assessment

  ○ Is there risk involved that needs analysis for more informed decision making?

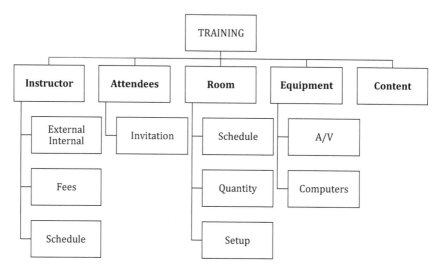

*Figure 5.11* Step 5: work breakdown structure example for training

- Selection matrix

  ○ What criteria is used to rate importance/priority (e.g., ROI, customer complaints, risk/safety, competition)?

- Resource allocation

  ○ Do you have the capacity internally? Can you free up someone temporarily?

- Assess other organizational initiatives (develop an operations work plan)

  ○ Have you identified all initiatives in one document to expose the entire organization's efforts? What are you expecting from I/T (for example) on the various initiatives at one time? What about marketing, facilities, and other support departments?

*Recommended reading for step 5*

Morris, Rick A. 2010. *Stop Playing Games! A Project Manager's Guide to Successfully Navigating Organizational Politics.* Minnetonka, MN: RMC Publications, Inc.
Ries, Eric. 2011. *The Lean Startup: How Today's Entrepreneurs Use Continuous Innovation to Create Radically Successful Businesses.* New York: Crown Business.
Whitten, Neal. 2005. *Neal Whitten's No-Nonsense Advice for Successful Projects.* Vienna, VA: Management Concepts.

### Step 6: develop action plan

Now that we understand priorities, we can start developing an action plan with a phased time line that accommodates the sequencing of initiatives. Steps 5 and 6,

*Table 5.1* Step 6: phased action plan

|  | PHASE 1<br>*1st Qtr* | PHASE 2<br>*2nd Qtr* | PHASE 3<br>*3rd Qtr* |
|---|:---:|:---:|:---:|
| **Strategy 1** | | | |
| PI 1A | | ✓ | |
| PI 1B | | ✓ | |
| **Strategy 2** | | | |
| PI 2A | ✓ | | |
| **Strategy 3** | | | |
| PI 3A | ✓ | | |
| PI 3B | | ✓ | |
| PI 3C | | | ✓ |
| **Strategy 4** | | | |
| PI 4A | | | ✓ |

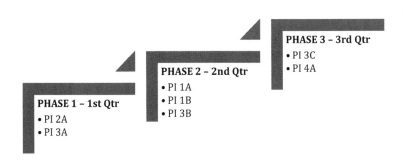

*Figure 5.12* Step 6: phased action plan sequence

prioritizing and sequencing, are often pushed downstream or, frankly, not done at all. I usually get presentation slides from executives of the strategic plan roll out and separately, disconnected, a list of improvement activities from quality or PI departments.

From a high level we look at sequencing the improvement initiatives and then phasing (see Table 5.1 and Figure 5.12). This communicates the message that you need to be held accountable to complete the phase 1 steps so that phase 2 can start on time. Execs know what is coming down the pike strategically and what they need to prepare for, so phasing should start with them.

**Step 6: action steps**

* Phased time line

    ○ What are the sequencing considerations?
    ○ What are the schedule impacts?
    ○ What are the resource issues?

### Step 7: communicate

Now here's the controversial step. It's just one word – communicate – but it is the step that requires a lot of reflection (like step 1). This is when we want to talk about 'transparency' – sharing the truth about the reality, where we need to get to, and asking for feedback. Remember Lean's focus on respect for people. How are we going to continuously improve, unless we respect and engage our experts?

Communication looks different when you are using strategy deployment:

> What we finally began to realize was that effective strategy deployment is really about engaging a conversation across the entire organization, from CEO to frontline.
>
> ". . . strategy deployment . . . requires leadership that is more facilitative, less authoritarian, less controlling, more team-based, and more willing to engage in dialogue."
>
> (ThedaCare Center for Healthcare Value 2011)

The A3 process (see step 4) is an excellent pathway for structured conversations.

### Step 7: action steps

- Get feedback before rolling out

*Recommended reading for step 7*

Balle, Michael and Freddy Balle. 2014. *Lead with Respect: A Novel of Lean Practice.* Cambridge: Lean Enterprise Institute.
ThedaCare Center for Healthcare Value. 2011. "Strategy Deployment." Accessed August 9, 2016. https://createvalue.org/wp-content/uploads/Strategy- Deployment_TCHV_ withQRC.pdf

### Step 8: make adjustments

If you are willing to receive feedback, the benefit is that adjustments can be made instead of having to say, "oops, we didn't think of that impact."

### Step 8: action steps

- New initiatives to add
- Re-sequence / re-prioritize

### Step 9: roll-out

We return to that powerful word: communicate. After getting feedback and making adjustments, we are ready now to roll-out the plan. Rolling out a plan using strategy deployment is more thoroughly vetted and with more than a few presentation slides that make you feel like you are expected to solve world hunger;

or the opposite: empty non-action words. There is often a disconnect between the executives and the front line where executives keep information close to the chest, and only give out nondescript 'go forth' messages. Too much time is wasted with staff trying to get more information, more clarity; we need to break down that barrier and work together on continuous improvement for the overall success of the business.

Don't misunderstand. Step 9 is not the final, complete set of activities, but it serves as the kickoff to the organization's focus and it gives direction. Now the improvement initiatives are ready to begin in concert with the strategic plan – a prioritization guide.

### Step 9: action steps

- Charter
- A3

  ○ Current state: value stream mapping and data collection
  ○ Root cause analysis: 5 whys, fishbone
  ○ Target condition: value stream mapping and measures

- Action plan for implementation
- Report outs

### *Step 10: assess process improvement in relation to the strategic plan*

As the details come forth, communication must be frequent in order to make any adjustments necessary to continue to make progress. Again, this is an iterative process.

Once the improvement initiatives get broken down further into manageable components by the 'experts' (the people doing the work), then more issues will come forth, creating offshoots of the large, strategically identified initiatives.

Consider the high-level action plan in step 6. If, for example, you have a new I/T implementation occurring in phase 3 (PI 3C), the phase 1 accountability would be to perform a work breakdown structure (as defined in step 5) so there is an understanding of what has to be done in phases 1 and 2 for a successful implementation in phase 3. I/T staff are not the only ones that need that information. How it impacts the rest of the organization and time commitments for training, etc., need to be known early on – to fully understand resource allocation, productivity issues, etc.

### Step 10: action steps

- Ensure measures are in line with outcomes and moving toward target
- Make adjustments
- Communicate frequently

## Conclusion

Creating a problem-solving culture supports strategy deployment. If we are all in this together, throughout all levels of the organization, we are transparent and know in which direction we need to head, we have more motivated staff to carry through, and they understand the value of their work and how it links to the strategic plan.

The following words of wisdom clearly state what is needed for policy (strategy) deployment – *hoshin kanri*:

> The idea is for top management to agree on a few simple goals for transitioning from mass to lean, to select a few projects to achieve these goals, to designate the people and resources for getting the projects done, and, finally to establish numerical improvement targets to be achieved by a given point in time.
>
> (Womack and Jones 2003, 95)

The clarity and simplicity of these words helps remind me how complicated we make things – too many strategic goals are unrealistic and unachievable based on their starting points and overextended resources. Yes, healthcare is a complex industry and as leaders we must provide focus and structure in order to pick up the pace of improving the right initiatives at the right time, to ensure that our strategic goals are actually achieved . . . faster.

## Bibliography

Dennis, Pascal. 2007. *Lean Production Simplified, Second Edition: A Plain Language Guide to the World's Most Powerful Production System.* Boca Raton, FL: CRC Press.

Lean Enterprise Institute. 2004. *Lean Lexicon: A Graphical Glossary for Lean Thinkers, Second Edition.* Cambridge: Lean Enterprise Institute.

Lewis, James P. 2001. *Project Planning, Scheduling, and Control,* Third Edition. New York: McGraw-Hill.

Manos, Anthony and Chad Vincent, editors. 2012. *The Lean Handbook.* Milwaukee, WI: ASQ Quality Press.

Morrill, Patricia. 2012. "Process Improvement Strategy Deployment." Copyright Registration Number TXu 1–846–033.

Morris, Rick A. 2010. *Stop Playing Games! A Project Manager's Guide to Successfully Navigating Organizational Politics.* Minnetonka, MN: RMC Publications, Inc.

ThedaCare Center for Healthcare Value. 2011. "Strategy Deployment." Accessed August 9, 2016. https://createvalue.org/wp-content/uploads/Strategy- Deployment_TCHV_withQRC.pdf

Womack, James P. and Daniel T. Jones. 2003. *Lean Thinking: Banish Waste and Create Wealth in Your Corporation.* New York: Free Press.

### *Recommended reading and research topics*

#### *Lean*

Graban, Mark. 2009. *Lean Hospitals: Improving Quality, Patient Safety, and Employee Satisfaction.* New York: Productivity Press.

Manos, Anthony and Chad Vincent, editors. 2012. *The Lean Handbook.* Milwaukee, WI: ASQ Quality Press.

Ries, Eric. 2011. *The Lean Startup: How Today's Entrepreneurs Use Continuous Innovation to Create Radically Successful Businesses.* New York: Crown Business.

Zidel, Thomas G. 2006. *A Lean Guide to Transforming Healthcare.* Milwaukee, WI: ASQ Quality Press.

## Metrics

Cunningham, Jean and Orest Fiume. 2003. *Real Numbers: Management Accounting in a Lean Organization.* Durham, NC: Managing Times Press.

Manos, Anthony and Chad Vincent, editors. 2012. *The Lean Handbook.* Milwaukee, WI: ASQ Quality Press.

## Project management

Lewis, James P. 2001. *Project Planning, Scheduling, and Control*, Third Edition. New York: McGraw-Hill.

Morris, Rick A. 2010. *Stop Playing Games! A Project Manager's Guide to Successfully Navigating Organizational Politics.* Minnetonka, MN: RMC Publications, Inc.

Whitten, Neal. 2005. *Neal Whitten's No-Nonsense Advice for Successful Projects.* Vienna, VA: Management Concepts.

## Respect

Balle, Michael and Freddy Balle. 2014. *Lead with Respect: A Novel of Lean Practice.* Cambridge: Lean Enterprise Institute.

## Strategic planning

Kenagy, John. 2009. *Designed to Adapt: Leading Healthcare in Challenging Times.* Bozeman, MT: Second River Healthcare Press.

McChesney, Chris, Sean Covey, and Jim Huling. 2012. *The 4 Disciplines of Execution: Achieving Your Wildly Important Goals.* New York: Simon & Schuster.

Ries, Eric. 2011. *The Lean Startup: How Today's Entrepreneurs Use Continuous Improvement to Create Radically Successful Businesses.* New York: Crown Business.

Toussaint, John and Roger A. Gerard. 2010. *On the Mend: Revolutionizing Healthcare to Save Lives and Transform the Industry.* Cambridge: Lean Enterprise Institute.

## Strategy, or policy, deployment, hoshin kanri

ThedaCare Center for Healthcare Value. 2011. "Strategy Deployment." Accessed August 9, 2016. https://createvalue.org/wp-content/uploads/Strategy- Deployment_TCHV_withQRC.pdf

Womack, James P. and Daniel T. Jones. 2003. *Lean Thinking: Banish Waste and Create Wealth in Your Corporation.* New York: Free Press.

## Value stream mapping

Rother, Mike and John Shook. 2009. *Learning to See: Value-Stream Mapping to Create Value and Eliminate Muda.* Cambridge: Lean Enterprise Institute.

# 6 Instruction on leading improvement

This chapter demonstrates how to use the case study in Part One, Chapter 1, to teach the 10-step model of *Process Improvement Strategy Deployment* (Morrill 2012) in Chapter Five.

## Case study patient scenarios

The following seven patient scenarios provide a brief synopsis of the case study in Chapter 1, highlighting each department. The last one is focused on the financial impact as exemplified in this case study. These are helpful during training and discussion of the steps involved in the *Process Improvement Strategy Deployment* model.

---

### Patient scenario: inpatient

Clara Wilson* was admitted to an inpatient unit after knee replacement surgery. It was not clear how long she would be on the unit, as they needed to watch her blood levels carefully as she had been taken off Coumadin (a blood thinner medication) for her surgery. They needed to watch for clots as they transitioned her back onto her medication regimen.

After a week on the unit, Clara was discharged via ambulance to the rehab facility for an expected two-week stay.

---

Clara was readmitted to the inpatient unit via the emergency department and was scheduled for a second knee surgery just three weeks after her discharge due to an infection.

She seemed to tolerate the surgery well and was discharged to the rehab hospital for another two-week stay.

---

After eight hours in the emergency department, Clara was admitted to an isolation room on the cardiac unit with a diagnosis of MRSA (from the knee replacement surgery) and congestive heart failure as well as a deep pressure ulcer on her left heel. Physicians treating her included infectious disease and cardiology. Her primary care physician was the attending.

Clara's daughter watched as a nurse gave her a shot in the stomach and asked if that was heparin (a blood thinner). Later, the daughter asked the doctor why she was on two blood thinners: heparin and Coumadin. The doctor responded that she didn't need to be on both.

After three days on the unit, it was determined that Clara experienced a cardiac event (after her second surgery) and the stent (inserted before her initial knee surgery) was no longer functioning as intended.

The orthopedic surgeon was apologetic about the MRSA and was eager to get her stabilized for surgery again so he could remove the knee prosthetic, allow the infection to resolve, then replace the prosthetic with another surgery in about six weeks. The other option presented to Clara to get rid of the MRSA was amputation.

The cardiologist indicated that Clara's heart would likely not withstand one, and definitely not two, more surgeries. She was at risk of dying on the operating table. Given these dismal options, Clara opted to go home with hospice care.

*Clara Wilson is not the patient's real name.

---

## Patient scenario: physician office visits

Clara Wilson* was referred to an orthopedic specialist for knee pain that was not resolved with cortisone injections. Clara met with the orthopedic surgeon who recommended knee replacement. Since Clara was under the care of several physicians, the specialist wanted a written release from three physicians that she was cleared for surgery.

Clara was provided forms to take to each physician for sign-off. Her cardiologist would not sign the release without a stress test. From the results of the stress test, the cardiologist scheduled a cardiac catheterization. He then scheduled a procedure for the following week to insert a stent.

Clara developed some problems at the site of the cardiac cath entry and returned to the cardiologist who then scheduled further tests for circulation in her leg. After those tests, Clara's primary care physician intervened and requested that further tests be delayed until after her knee replacement surgery, as that was the primary need at the time.

The cardiologist subsequently signed off and Clara was cleared for knee replacement surgery – a full four months after her initial orthopedic visit.

The orthopedic specialist then ordered an MRI for design of the knee prosthetic.

---

Clara Wilson was visited by her primary care physician in the hospital after her knee replacement surgery. They discussed Clara's options for rehab facilities once she was discharged.

---

Clara's physician received updates from the rehab facility but was never seen there by her primary. She was under the care of the facility's physician who saw her only twice.

---

When Clara was admitted to the hospital for the third time, her physician was the attending and was on rotation for the first three days of the hospitalization. After that, a partner from the office (on hospital rotation) took over Clara's case.

---

When Clara was discharged to her home with hospice care, her primary care physician visited her twice after office hours and was updated on Clara's case by the hospice physician.

---

Clara died six weeks after being discharged from the hospital.

*Clara Wilson is not the patient's real name.

---

## Patient scenario: rehab

Clara Wilson* was transferred via ambulance from an inpatient unit to the rehab hospital following knee replacement surgery.

Clara handled the rehab routine well though she developed a pressure ulcer on her left heel.

After two weeks, Clara was discharged to her home with a referral for home care services. Clara's daughter was scheduled to be with Clara to assist her the first week she came home.

Clara received physical therapy, occupational therapy, and nursing visits in the home. The nurse dressed the pressure ulcer, which continued to worsen.

After one week at home, Clara experienced excruciating pain in her knee and was unable to walk.

Clara was taken to the emergency department.

---

Clara returned to the rehab facility after her second knee surgery to begin the rehab routine a second time for an expected two-week stay.

Clara had a fever and her pressure ulcer continued to worsen. Also, her knee began to drain at the incision site. An infectious disease specialist was called in for a consult.

After one week, Clara was transported to the emergency department with the diagnosis of kidney failure.

*Clara Wilson is not the patient's real name.

## Patient scenario: emergency

Clara Wilson* was transported via ambulance to the emergency department from the rehab facility, where she was recovering from a second knee surgery due to a hospital-acquired infection (MRSA). Clara had a fever and the staff at the rehab facility diagnosed her with possible kidney failure.

Clara's family arrived to be with her, however, only one person could be with her at a time because she was placed in the hallway with other patients because there were no rooms available.

Tests were performed and after eight hours in the emergency department, Clara was admitted to an isolation room on the cardiac unit with a diagnosis of congestive heart failure. Her kidneys were functioning properly.

*Clara Wilson is not the patient's real name.

## Patient scenario: surgery

Clara Wilson* was scheduled for knee replacement surgery after three of her physicians had to sign-off that she was cleared for surgery.

Clara appropriately prepared for surgery by discontinuing her Coumadin (blood thinner medication).

The surgery was considered a success but it was unclear how long she would remain in the hospital as they wanted to carefully manage Clara's blood levels to avoid clotting.

Clara was discharged to a rehab facility for an expected two-week stay. She was transported via ambulance to the facility.

---

Clara returned to surgery three weeks after knee replacement. This second surgery (irrigation and debridement) was scheduled to clean out the area.

After inpatient care, she was discharged to the rehab hospital again for two weeks.

---

After ten days, Clara's orthopedic surgeon recommended a third surgery to remove the knee prosthesis to allow the MRSA to resolve and then a fourth surgery six weeks later to replace the prosthesis.

The other option was amputation.

Clara's cardiologist indicated that Clara would most likely die on the operating table as her heart was too weak for any more surgeries.

*Clara Wilson is not the patient's real name.

## Patient scenario: nutrition

After eight hours in the emergency department, Clara Wilson* was admitted to an isolation room on the cardiac unit with a diagnosis of MRSA (following knee replacement surgery) and congestive heart failure as well as a deep pressure ulcer on her left heel.

Clara had difficulty swallowing and the doctor ordered soft foods for her. She later experienced pain when drinking or eating anything cold. Clara's daughters requested that the doctor change the dietary order from soft food to whatever Clara could tolerate.

Each morning, someone from Nutrition Services came to Clara's room to talk with her about menu selections. Clara and her two daughters discussed the choices and made the food requests for the next three meals.

Each time the meal tray was brought to Clara, it did not contain any of the food or beverage requested. The nurses on the cardiac unit made soup and decaf coffee for Clara.

Clara's daughters asked repeatedly why the food requested was never what was brought to the room. The Nutrition Services staff said they would check on it. The nurses on the cardiac unit said they would check on it. The doctor indicated she had changed the dietary order.

After Clara had been on the cardiac unit for five days, the nurse manager stopped by to see Clara and ask if things were going okay with her stay on the unit. Clara and her daughters expressed their frustration with meals. He said he would check on that.

*Clara Wilson is not the patient's real name.

## Patient scenario: financial services/patient accounts

Clara Wilson* was scheduled for knee replacement surgery. She was covered by Medicare with AARP as a secondary payer.

She was readmitted to the hospital three weeks after surgery and had a second knee surgery due to infection.

Clara returned for a third hospitalization after an eight-hour length of stay in the emergency department. She was discharged to home with hospice care.

———————

Medicare may investigate, reduce, or deny payments for charges related to the following:

- Pressure ulcer
- Hospital-acquired infection
- Readmissions

*Clara Wilson is not the patient's real name.

# GROUP ACTIVITY FOR STEPS 1–4 OF *PROCESS IMPROVEMENT STRATEGY DEPLOYMENT* – APPROXIMATELY 30–40 MINUTES TOTAL

*Part 1* (15–20 minutes)

With a large group (24–50) or a small group (10–24), divide them into two teams (per table if a large group or separate tables if a small group) after working through steps 1–4 of the *Process Improvement Strategy Deployment* model.

## Team A: patient scenario

Give each table one of the patient scenarios. If the participants cannot relate from a professional perspective, encourage them to think about the scenario happening to a loved one.

During this activity, Team A is to answer the following:

1   What are your observations about the issues that need improvement in the scenarios?
2   Now relate those issues to the organizationwide strategic planning process:

What are three or four themes that encompass the issues to raise to a strategic level?

## Team B: strategic plan

Use the strategic plan form for Team B that follows.

During this activity, instruct Team B participants as follows:
1   Consider yourselves members of the executive team.
2   Your team has already identified the five strategic goals as listed under "Strategic Plan for Team B."
3   Identify what strategies and/or tactics are needed.

*Part 2* (15–20 minutes)

## Teams A and B together

1   Team B: Share your strategic plan information with Team A.
2   Team A: How well do your themes match the strategic plan?
3   Are there any changes you wish to make together to the strategic goals?

# STRATEGIC PLAN FOR TEAM B

1   Embed a patient-centered culture throughout the organization.
2   Develop external partnerships for continuum of care.
3   Reduce waste and cost in operational processes.
4   Grow the orthopedic service line.

5 Reinvent the food service brand for healthy meals to inpatients and employees.

Strategies and/or tactics:

_____

_____

_____

_____

_____

_____

_____

_____

_____

_____

## GROUP ACTIVITY FOR STEPS 5–8 OF *PROCESS IMPROVEMENT STRATEGY DEPLOYMENT* – APPROXIMATELY 20 MINUTES

After working through steps 5–8, have the same table teams as in the previous activity work together to "develop action plan/phased time line" (see Figure 6.1).
Instruct participants to work on the following:

1 How would you prioritize process improvement initiatives given the organizational strategic direction?

    a Take the strategic plan goals you may have altered
    b Break them down into manageable components
    c Look for sequencing and number them
    d Develop a phased time line

**Develop action plan/phased time line for teams A and B together**

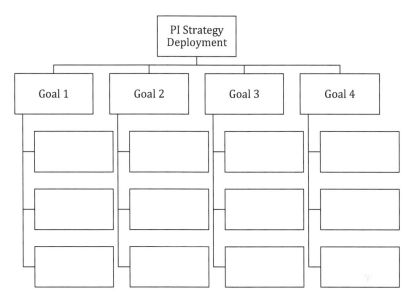

*Figure 6.1* Group activity steps 5–8

## Application example of the 10-step model using the case study events in part one, Chapter 1

### *Step 1: ensure high-level understanding of current state*

Start a high-level value stream map for knee replacement surgery encountered in Chapter 1 (see Figure 6.2). More detail can be added (as shown) for a better understanding of the multiple players involved.

### *Step 2: develop strategic plan*

The current-state assessment, including observation and value stream mapping, can then serve as valuable input for your strategic planning sessions.

Using the strategic goals identified in the group activity for steps 1–4, the next step is to clearly identify accountability (see Figure 6.3).

### *Step 3: set target measures*

The executives identified need to take a deeper dive into their areas of account-ability to understand current state and best practice indicators to begin to draft the target measures and prepare the gap analysis (see Figure 6.4).

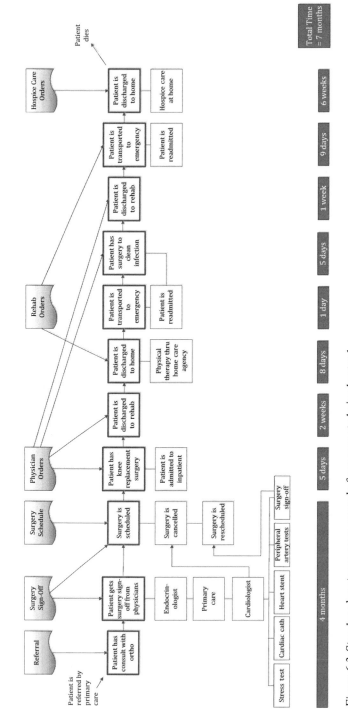

*Figure 6.2* Step 1: value stream map example from case study in chapter 1

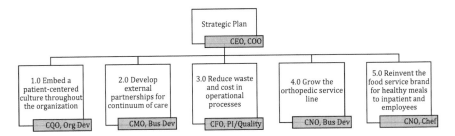

*Figure 6.3* Step 2: strategic plan goals example from case study in chapter 1

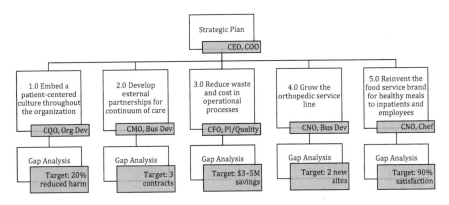

*Figure 6.4* Step 3: target measures example from case study in chapter 1

### *Step 4: Identify key process improvement initiatives*

With the information gathered so far, the executives can begin their project charter (see Figure 6.5).

The high-level project charter can then help executives initiate several A3 problem-solving tools (see Figure 6.6) with the following 'Problem/Issue':

- A3.1: inconsistent clinical care (preventable harm): orthopedic surgical site infections
- A3.2: inconsistent clinical care (preventable harm): pressure ulcers
- A3.3: inconsistent clinical care (preventable harm): medication errors
- A3.4: lacking interdisciplinary, coordinated orthopedic care teams
- A3.5: orthopedic pre-op education may need to be more comprehensive

**Project Charter: Strategic Plan 4.0 Grow the Orthopedic Service Line**

**Business Case:** In order to stay competitive in our core business of orthopedics, we need to expand our geographic reach. This Strategic Plan Goal involves investigation of two additional locations to meet increasing demand for orthopedic surgeries and related care.

| Problem/Opportunity: | Scope, Constraints, Assumptions: |
|---|---|
| (1) Inconsistent clinical care outcomes (preventable harm): surgical site infections, pressure ulcers, medication errors<br>(2) Lacking interdisciplinary, coordinated care teams<br>(3) What is included in pre-op education (including risk and consent)? May need to be more comprehensive.<br>(4) Declining market share with increasing orthopedic demand<br>(5) Patients travel long distance for services | • Current clinical care outcomes need improvement before we expand services.<br>• Business plan development. It is assumed that two zip codes consistently identified in the market share report indicate some volume and may present opportunities for growth – even before new locations.<br>• Business development and facility planning can investigate (confidentially) additional sites while the clinical improvement effort is underway.<br>• Physician recruitment is not included in the scope. |

| Goal: | Stakeholders: |
|---|---|
| (1) Develop an interdisciplinary, coordinated care team model for the orthopedic service line<br>(2) Increase market share within one year<br>(3) Open two additional locations within three years | Orthopedic physicians, rehab leadership, nurse educator, chief medical officer |
| | **Team:**<br>Executive Sponsor: CNO<br>Physician Champion:<br>Facilitator:<br>Team Members:<br>Ad Hoc Members: |

| Preliminary Project Plan | Target Dates / Budget | Actual Dates / Budget |
|---|---|---|
| Investigate and develop a clinical care improvement plan focusing on: (1) interdisciplinary, coordinated care teams and (2) preventable harm. | Qtr 1: Improvement Planning with stakeholders & team development<br>Qtr 2 – 4: Phased A3 Problem Solving & Implementation | |
| Develop business plan for orthopedic service line growth. | Qtr 2 | |
| Investigate additional sites | Qtr 3 – 4 | |

| Prepared by: | Approved by: |
|---|---|
| | CNO and Business Development Executive |

*Figure 6.5* Step 4: project charter example from case study in chapter 1

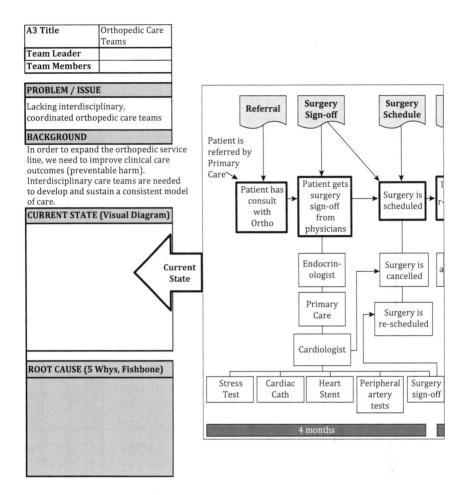

| A3 Title | Orthopedic Care Teams |
|---|---|
| Team Leader | |
| Team Members | |

**PROBLEM / ISSUE**

Lacking interdisciplinary, coordinated orthopedic care teams

**BACKGROUND**

In order to expand the orthopedic service line, we need to improve clinical care outcomes (preventable harm). Interdisciplinary care teams are needed to develop and sustain a consistent model of care.

**CURRENT STATE (Visual Diagram)**

Current State

**ROOT CAUSE (5 Whys, Fishbone)**

Referral

Surgery Sign-off

Surgery Schedule

Patient is referred by Primary Care

Patient has consult with Ortho

Patient gets surgery sign-off from physicians

Surgery is scheduled

Endocrin-ologist

Surgery is cancelled

Primary Care

Surgery is re-scheduled

Cardiologist

| Stress Test | Cardiac Cath | Heart Stent | Peripheral artery tests | Surgery sign-off |

4 months

*Figure 6.6* Step 4: A3 problem-solving example from case study in chapter 1

### Step 5: prioritize process improvement initiatives

From the project charter, use the 'preliminary project plan' to start the high-level work breakdown structure (see Figures 6.7 and 6.8).

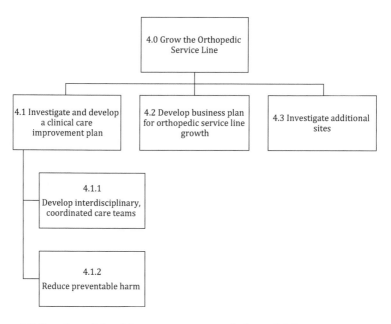

*Figure 6.7* Step 5: work breakdown structure example for goal 4.0

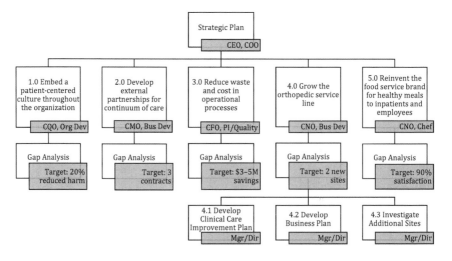

*Figure 6.8* Step 5: strategic plan goals with work breakdown structure example for goal 4.0

### Step 6: develop action plan (see strategy 4 example in **Table 6.1**)

*Table 6.1* Step 6: phased action plan example for goal 4.0

|  | PHASE 1<br>*1st Qtr* | PHASE 2<br>*2nd Qtr* | PHASE 3<br>*3rd Qtr* |
|---|---|---|---|
| **4.0**<br>**Orthopedic**<br>**Service Line**<br>**Growth** |  |  |  |
| PI 4.1<br>Investigate and develop a<br>clinical care improvement plan | ✓ | ✓ |  |
| PI 4.2<br>Develop business plan for<br>orthopedic service line growth |  | ✓ | ✓ |
| PI 4.3<br>Investigate additional sites |  | ✓ | ✓ |

### Steps 7 and 8: communicate and make adjustments

Be sure to test this plan with the appropriate individuals before rolling it out to check for any omissions or sequencing adjustments based on other organizational efforts underway.

### Step 9: roll-out

You now have more meaningful information for every level of the organization to grasp and remember: the areas of focus for the year and who the leads are. This enables each employee to begin to understand how his or her work links to the strategic plan – how he or she adds value to the organization. Identifying the leads with each initiative helps co-workers understand the additional work effort others will have. This might even spark the desire to offer help!

**Now go forth and teach others** *Process Improvement Strategy Deployment* **(see Figure 6.9).**

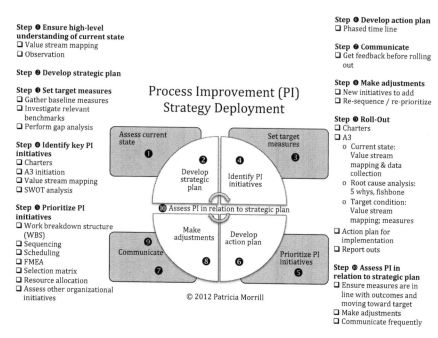

Step ❶ Ensure high-level understanding of current state
❑ Value stream mapping
❑ Observation

Step ❷ Develop strategic plan

Step ❸ Set target measures
❑ Gather baseline measures
❑ Investigate relevant benchmarks
❑ Perform gap analysis

Step ❹ Identify key PI initiatives
❑ Charters
❑ A3 initiation
❑ Value stream mapping
❑ SWOT analysis

Step ❺ Prioritize PI initiatives
❑ Work breakdown structure (WBS)
❑ Sequencing
❑ Scheduling
❑ FMEA
❑ Selection matrix
❑ Resource allocation
❑ Assess other organizational initiatives

Step ❻ Develop action plan
❑ Phased time line

Step ❼ Communicate
❑ Get feedback before rolling out

Step ❽ Make adjustments
❑ New initiatives to add
❑ Re-sequence / re-prioritize

Step ❾ Roll-Out
❑ Charters
❑ A3
  o Current state: Value stream mapping & data collection
  o Root cause analysis: 5 whys, fishbone
  o Target condition: Value stream mapping; measures
❑ Action plan for implementation
❑ Report outs

Step ❿ Assess PI in relation to strategic plan
❑ Ensure measures are in line with outcomes and moving toward target
❑ Make adjustments
❑ Communicate frequently

Process Improvement (PI) Strategy Deployment

© 2012 Patricia Morrill

*Figure 6.9  Process Improvement Strategy Deployment* 10-step model

# Bibliography

Morrill, Patricia. 2012. "Process Improvement Strategy Deployment." Copyright Registration Number TXu 1–846–033.Table 3.1  Assessment of current state: care coordination.

# Index

Printed and bound by CPI Group (UK) Ltd, Croydon, CR0 4YY

21/10/2024

01777055-0019